U.S.MAIL.
2nd Corps.

Brothers in Arms

BROTHERS IN ARMS

THE LIVES AND EXPERIENCES OF THE MEN
WHO FOUGHT THE CIVIL WAR – IN THEIR OWN WORDS

WILLIAM C. DAVIS

A Salamander Book

This edition published in 1995 by SMITHMARK Publishers Inc., 16 East 32nd Street, New York, NY 10016.

1 2 3 4 5 6 7 8 9

SMITHMARK books are available for bulk purchase for sales promotion and premium use. For details write or call the manager of special sales, SMITHMARK Publishers Inc., 16 East 32nd Street, New York, NY 10016; (212) 532-6600.

ISBN 0-8317-0768-2

Printed in Italy

All correspondence concerning this volume should be addressed to Salamander Books Limited, 129-137 York Way, London N7 9LG, England.

Credits

Editor: Tony Hall
Designer: Paul Johnson
Headline calligraphy: Andrew Whiteley, The Inkshed, London
Filmsetting: SX Composing, Rayleigh, Essex
Color reproduction: PixelTech. Prepress PTE., Singapore

Introduction

"How strange it is. We have been united in our views of almost all subjects, public and private. We still have, I trust, a personal regard for each other, which will continue whatever course our sense of duty may dictate, yet in one short year after exchanging at your house assurances of friendship, here we are, face to face, with arms in our hands, with every prospect of bloody collision. How strange."

Confederate General Braxton Bragg to Union General Henry Hunt, 1861

The uniform and personal belongings of General George G. Meade. Meade's military career prior to the war was typical of so many professional soldiers of the period: education at West Point and service on the frontier and in the Mexican War. It was a pattern that would be followed by many of the senior commanders both North and South.
Artifacts courtesy of: The Civil War Library and Museum, Philadelphia, Pa.

It was all going to be such fun. The people of America rushed to war on a wave of patriotic fever and a belief that it would all be over in a matter of weeks. Like these volunteers of 1861, they had no idea of the horrors they were about to bring down on themselves.

All across America, North and South, beneath the excitement and euphoria, the fear and uncertainty, most people felt that same sense of "how strange" it was. Indeed, though the tensions that brought them to the brink of war had been tugging at them for generations, still at the end it all seemed to have happened so fast. The country, it seemed, had lost its mind and turned to strike itself.

As always, it was chiefly the politicians who had failed, stumbling in their way, blinded by sectional and personal interests, mindless of the long range impact of what they did as they sought some immediate goal and power. Inevitably, when their blundering, compounded by facing problems like slavery and the nature of the Union that did not offer easy solutions, finally led the country to war's precipice, it was out of their hands. They *made* the

It didn't take very long for America to realise what its war would mean. As the armies grew, so did the numbers of dead and wounded.

The uniforms and personal belongings of John Hunt Morgan; one of the Confederacy's finest cavalry commanders. Like so many, he would choose his side and live and die by the decision.
Artifacts courtesy of: The Museum of the Confederacy, Richmond, Va.

war to come, but it would be the innocent, the farmboys and students and clerks who would have to *fight* it, and it would be their families behind the lines who would suffer the shortages and the uncertainty, and ultimately the loss of loved ones.

Ahead of those men – white and black and red, native and foreign born, young and old, and even a few women who *seemed* to be men – ahead of all of them lay four years they would never forget, and that posterity would not let die. They chose their sides and followed their warring causes, yet first to last there was always more to bind than separate them. They shared the same experiences, North and South, faced the same dangers, sang the same songs, laughed at the same stories. Blue or gray, when they were wounded and dying, their blood was always red. That, as much as anything, created a bond that mere factional politics could not sunder. *That* is what made them Brothers in Arms.

CHAPTER ONE

Nothing left now but to fight

Inevitably it had come, as so many of them had feared it would. Generations of argument, accusation, and arrogance, finally brought North and South to the war table, and before it was over, millions of men would sit at the tragic feast. Overwhelmingly they were men who had nothing at all to do with bringing on the conflict. The politicians had done that, as usual, but it would be left to the farm boys, the clerks, the students, the mechanics, to risk their blood and their futures to decide the contest.

Ahead of them lay four years of hardship and sacrifice, laced as well with fun, humor, adventure, and the overwhelming sense of participating in something larger than themselves. It was to be the great event of their generation, and the defining experience of their century. Indeed, in the end it bound them all, North and South, into a fraternity initiated in mutual triumph and tragedy. Regardless of the color of their uniforms, they were to be the makers of America's future.

The Confederacy would experiment with several flag patterns during the war. This one, the First National, was one of its most famous, the so-called "Stars and Bars."
Artifact courtesy of: The Museum of the Confederacy, Richmond, Va.

Kentucky State Guard members in 1860, with the war only months ahead of them. Most would become Confederate soldiers in the famous First Kentucky or "Orphan" Brigade. Most of them would never see home again.

> "A CRISIS IN MY LIFE [IS] AT HAND. MY PEOPLE ARE GOING TO WAR, AND WAR FOR THEIR LIBERTY. IF I DON'T COME AND BEAR MY PART THEY WILL BELIEVE ME A COWARD – AND I WILL FEEL THAT I AM OCCUPYING THE POSITION OF ONE. I MUST GO AND STAND MY CHANCES."
>
> *Lieutenant Edward Porter Alexander of Georgia, on his decision to join the Southern Confederacy*

The young men who went off to war tried as best they could to take their families with them, certainly in their hearts, and often in these cased ambrotypes of wives and children.
Artifacts courtesy of: The Museum of the Confederacy, Richmond, Va.

The boys went off to war in all manner of uniforms and regalia, some of it distinctly un-regulation. This New Englander wears local Indian decoration over his uniform, symbolic perhaps of his blood. Certainly it was to be everyone's war.

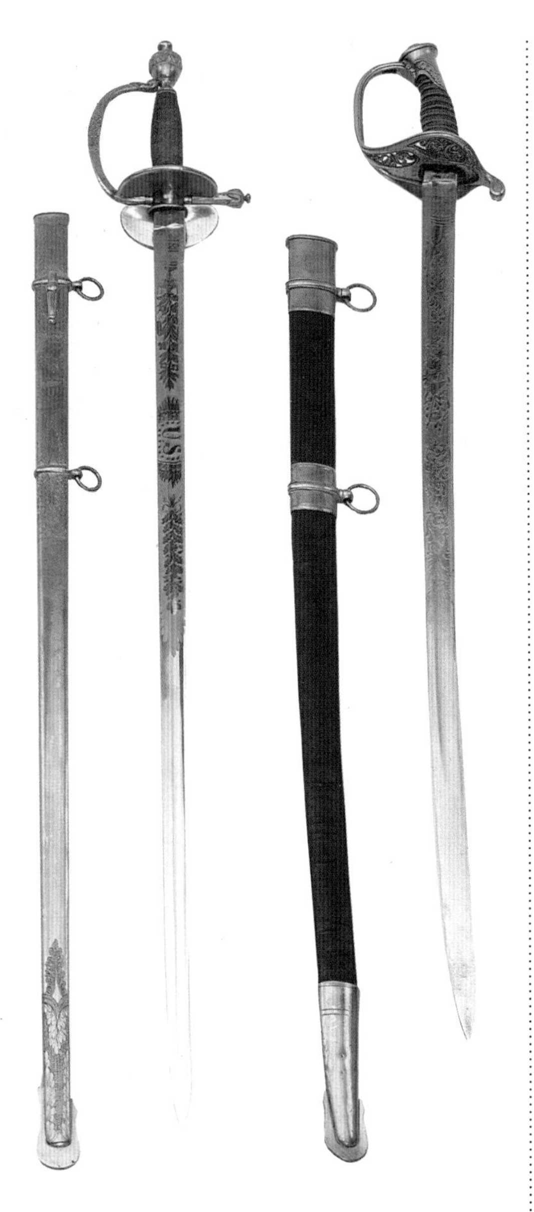

The pre-war Regulars who made their choices in 1860 used sabers like the 1840 pattern foot officer's sword at left, and the 1850 pattern at right. Their old weapons symbolized their attitudes toward what the war would become.
Artifacts courtesy of: The Civil War Library and Museum, Philadelphia, Pa.

When war erupted in Charleston Harbor on April 12, 1861, the entire United States Army – what would soon be called the 'Old Army' – numbered a bare 13,000 or more men on active duty, most of them scattered across thousands of square miles of frontier posts west of the Mississippi. Service in the Regulars may well have made a gentleman of an officer, and bound him and his fellows together in long-held relationships of affection and trust, but the men in the ranks enjoyed little of such. They had often as not been the poor of their communities, taking on the uniform because there was nothing else for them to do, while many more were recent immigrants, especially Irish and Germans, taking the only profession they could get.

The coming of the war would change life for all of them. The Old Army, in its way, mirrored the dividing nation itself, and the greatest battles these professionals would fight would be not on the battlefield, but in their own hearts in a war between duty and loyalty.

Scattered all across the continent at frontier posts like this one in the New Mexico territory, the Old Army officers and soldiers were mostly far removed from the events in the East that precipitated the outbreak of war.

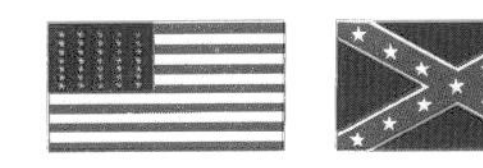

When the guns began to sound here at Fort Sumter in April 1861, the days of waiting were over. Everyone had to make his choice of side. Typically, it was Old Army officers who commanded on both sides as the fort was besieged.

The 1858 pattern US Army hat, often called the Jeff Davis or Hardee hat, with some of the brass badges worn on it to denote branch of service.
Artifacts courtesy of: West Point Museum, West Point, NY.

> "A COMPANY OF SOLDIERS, AFTER THEY HAVE SERVED TOGETHER FOR SOME MONTHS, BECOME LIKE A LARGE FAMILY . . . WE SOON KNEW EACH OTHER'S GOOD POINTS, FAILINGS AND WEAKNESSES."
>
> *Augustus Meyers, Musician, United States Army (USA), 1850s*

> **"SO IMPATIENT DID I BECOME FOR STARTING THAT I FELT LIKE TEN THOUSAND PINS WERE PRICKING ME IN EVERY PART OF THE BODY, AND STARTED OFF A WEEK IN ADVANCE OF MY BROTHERS."**
>
> *Frank Peak, Confederate soldier*

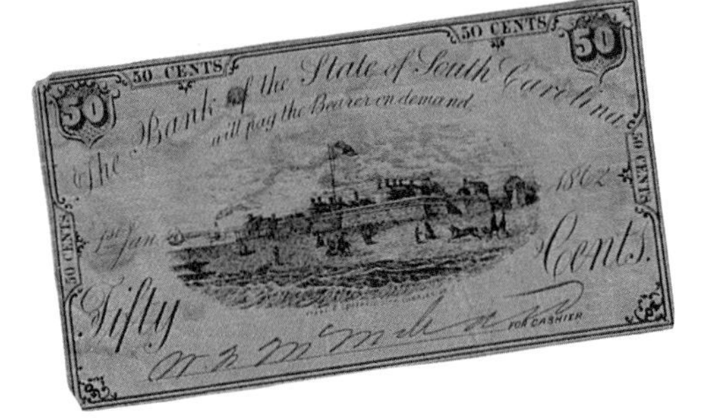

A fifty cent note on the Bank of South Carolina. As hopeful as the enthusiastic young "Southrons" who flocked to the Confederate banners after Fort Sumter, Southern currency was just as fragile, backed by little more than courage.
Artifact courtesy of: The Museum of the Confederacy, Richmond, Va.

Northerners, too, rushed to arms in the wake of Sumter, and every city and county town square witnessed scenes like this in Michigan as one of its first regiments prepares to leave for the front.

They identified with their brave banners, like this Virginia State Seal flag from an unknown Old Dominion regiment. "Ever thus to tyrants," its Latin motto proclaimed.
Artifact courtesy of: The Museum of the Confederacy, Richmond, Va.

So proudly did the soldiers regard their flags that they used them to boast of their battles. Regiments North and South emblazoned their battle honors on their colors and guidons.

No sooner had the first guns echoed over Fort Sumter than a wave of enthusiasm swept North and South. Across the new Confederacy young men rushed to enlist, and state governors at first had to turn away volunteers for want of sufficient arms and uniforms. In the old Union, men of all stripes came forward as well, intent on avenging the insult to Old Glory. Indeed, though their causes might differ, the reactions of the young American men on either side of the Mason-Dixon Line were much the same. A visitor in North Carolina found that the crowds screamed so loud that they drowned out the bands playing 'Dixie.' Eyes blazed, every voice shouted, mothers proudly urged their sons to enlist, and sweethearts threatened rejection of those boys who quailed from the fight. 'I was a mere boy and carried away by boyish enthusiasm,' wrote a Tennessee Confederate. 'I was tormented by feverish anxiety before I joined my regiment for fear the fighting would be over before I got into it.'

To accompany their colors, every regiment had either a band, or at least a drummer and bugler, like this musician from a Confederate North Carolina unit.

Little Johnny Clem, the "drummer boy of Shiloh," symbolized the youngsters who wanted to see the war despite being under age.

Women, too, wanted to share the experience. The soldier seated at right is Private Albert Cashier, or so his companion thought. In fact, it is Jenny Hodgers, who kept up her masquerade through the whole war.

> "AH, CAPT. REDDISH! I ONLY WISH YOU HAD A HUNDRED SUCH FINE BOYS AS THIS ONE! HE'S ALL RIGHT, AND GOOD FOR THE SERVICE."
>
> *Surgeon Leonidas Clemmons, 61st Illinois Infantry*

The standard infantry officer's forage cap often called a McDowell cap after unlucky General Irvin McDowell. McDowell's Union army was routed at the war's first major battle at Manassas.

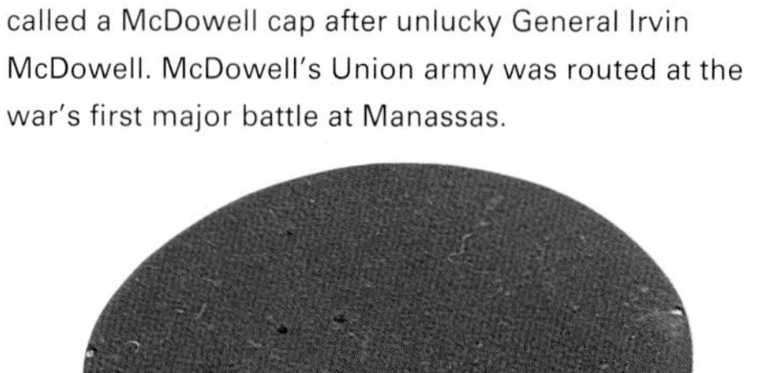

Young Johnny Rebs and Billy Yanks had no idea of what to expect when they went to the recruiting sergeant, signed their name or made their mark, and undertook to become soldiers. Some got a slap on the back and a handshake from their future officers, others got a drink or a fine feast, and still more proudly displayed their enlistment papers to a swarm of applauding and fluttering girls. Brass marching bands accompanied groups of hopeful volunteers from the village square to the recruiter, then serenaded them on to the hastily erected induction camps. An almost religious fervor could sweep the crowd, with men caught up in the rush of patriotism by the speeches and the songs, surging forward to sign their names. Lifelong friends volunteered together, and whole school classes sometimes closed that the students could take the uniform. Everyone wanted to be a soldier, and when surgeons like Clemmons gave their cursory examinations, men missing fingers and eyes, with weak lungs and hearts, and occasionally even a disguised woman, passed the physical.

At first, both sides imported large numbers of rifles to arm their regiments, including the British 1853 Enfield at top with its triangular bayonet, and the Belgian 1842 pattern rifle below, equipped with a saber-bayonet.
Artifacts courtesy of: Virginia Historical Society, Richmond, Va.

> "HANCOCK, GOOD-BY; YOU CAN NEVER KNOW WHAT THIS HAS COST ME, AND I HOPE GOD WILL STRIKE ME DEAD IF I AM EVER INDUCED TO LEAVE MY NATIVE SOIL, SHOULD WORSE COME TO WORST."
>
> *Lewis A. Armistead, 1861, on leaving the Old Army for the Confederacy*

General Braxton Bragg had a long career in the Old Army, going back to the Mexican War in the 1840s. Ironically, one of his close friends in 1861 was William T. Sherman, later commander of the Union's Army of the Tennessee.

In early 1861 Lincoln offered command of the Union Army to Robert E. Lee, but the Virginian felt other tugs of loyalty that drew him inexorably toward the gray.

Armistead spoke for many career soldiers from the South who, when the war came, found that their loyalty to their native states overrode their old devotion to the Union. Of the 1,000 officers or so serving in the Old Army when the war came, more than a third of them resigned to join the Confederacy, including one of only four field generals. The choice was a wrenching one to make. Most had spent all their adult lives in the Union uniform defending the constitution they were now on course to attack. What is more most of their oldest and closest friends were fellow officers who came from the North. They knew no other life, no other home.

As a result, Henry Heth, on leaving for the Confederacy, confessed that 'no act of my life cost me more bitter pangs than mailing my resignation.' And Colonel Robert E. Lee of Virginia, offered command of the entire United States Army at the outbreak of war in in 1861, had to turn down a soldier's ultimate dream rather than betray and fight his fellow Virginians.

The coat of the 18th New York's drum major at left; the 129th Pennsylvania's officer's coat next to it, and the 51st New York Militia's coat at right.
Artifacts courtesy of: West Point Museum, West Point, NY.

Many an officer carried one of Samuel Colt's revolver designs, from the model 1860 "Army" .44 pistol at top, to the 1849 "pocket" model below.
Artifacts courtesy of: The Museum of the Confederacy, Richmond, Va.

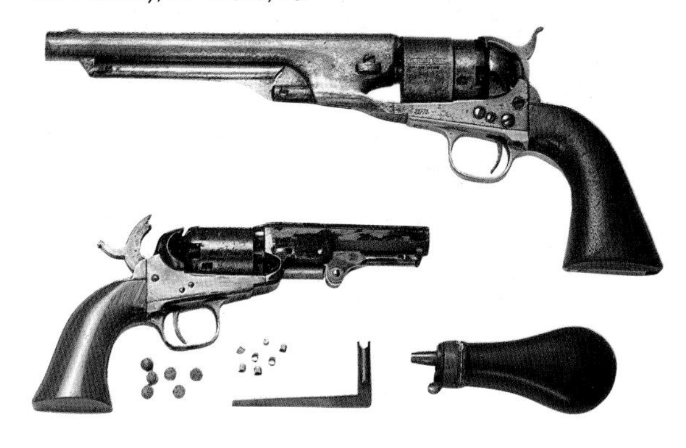

The outbreak of war did not just cause the breakup of old friendships. It actually tore families apart. General Philip St. George Cooke of the Union cavalry had two sons in the Confederate Army, one of them a general, and one son-in-law, General "Jeb" Stuart. The entire family of the Union's first lady, Mary Todd Lincoln, adhered to the South. Two of her brothers died in Confederate uniform, and her brother-in-law the Confederate General Ben Hardin Helm was killed in action. General James B. Terrill of Virginia wore the gray while his brother General William Terrill wore the blue, and Thomas Crittenden of Kentucky became a Union general in the same theater of the war where his brother George was a general for the Confederacy.

The lowly enlisted man felt it, too. In 1863 at Gettysburg, in the fighting for Culp's Hill, a casualty was Wesley Culp, who left Pennsylvania to join the South and came back to die almost on his own farm. Many a family never reconciled again, even after the war was long over.

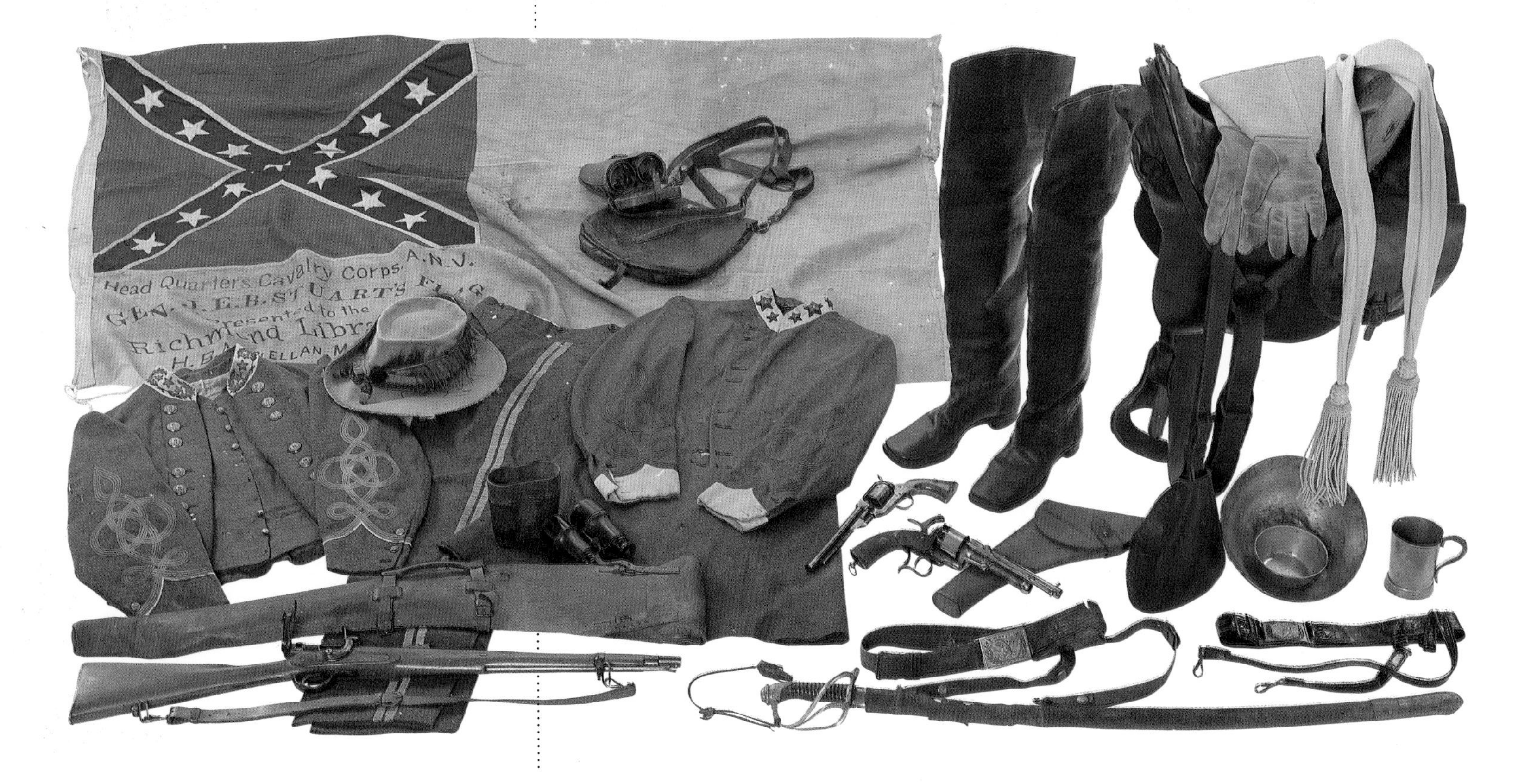

Symbolic of the sundered families split by the war, the flag and personal effects of General James E. B. "Jeb" Stuart pay testimony to one great Confederate whose father-in-law and one brother-in-law fought for the Union.
Artifacts courtesy of: The Museum of the Confederacy, Richmond, Va., and the Virginia Historical Society, Richmond, Va.

For all too many families, only death reunited the sons and fathers and brothers whom war had separated. This Confederate lived through four years of fighting, to die in the last weeks at Petersburg, Virginia, in 1865.

"Jeb" Stuart came to represent the very ideal of the bold, dashing cavalryman North and South. Until his death in 1864 at the battle of Yellow Tavern north of Richmond, he made life a nightmare for the Union, including his own father-in-law.

"BE CONSOLED BY THE REFLECTION THAT YOUR HUSBAND & BROTHERS WILL ATONE FOR THE FATHER'S CONDUCT."

General "Jeb" Stuart, Confederate States Army (CSA), 1861, on his father-in-law staying with the Union

They went to war in an era when the trappings of war were colorful and shining. Even their buttons proclaimed their allegiances. These Yankee buttons range from those of the US Military Academy, to those worn by members of the diplomatic corps. *Artifacts courtesy of: William L. Leigh Collection, Chantilly, Va.*

As soon as the guns began to sound – indeed, months before – other Americans felt the tug of patriotism. Slavery was what had brought North and South to blows, and in both sections blacks, both free and slave, wanted to participate in the struggle that would decide the fate of the Union and of their race in America.

Surprisingly, the first outpourings came in the South, where free blacks like those in Petersburg, Virginia, asked to be allowed to volunteer. Even some slaves hoped to take part, but only in 1865, with the war almost done, would the Confederacy countenance such enlistments.

While only a fraction of Negroes supported the Confederacy, blacks overwhelmingly backed the North to fight for freedom, respect, and a place in society. They had to fight prejudice and suspicion for years before finally they could fight the Confederacy. But in the end over 185,000 of them wore the blue, and in 1864–65 mixed their blood with their white comrades on the battlefields of the South.

Not surprisingly, in a war brought about by slavery, the blacks themselves wanted to have a part. Confederate Negroes never served in great numbers, but more than 100,000 free blacks and former slaves took arms for the Union.

This Model 1842 musket hit by a 6 lb. solid cannon ball was recovered from a Virginia battlefield.
Artifacts courtesy of: Wendell Lang Collection, Tarrytown, NY.

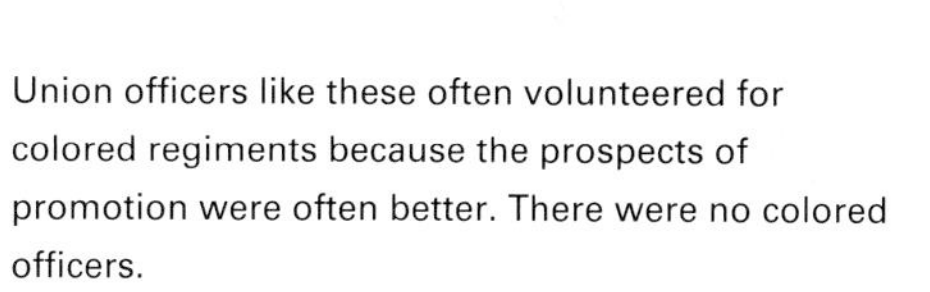

Union officers like these often volunteered for colored regiments because the prospects of promotion were often better. There were no colored officers.

"IN OUR NEIGHBORING CITY OF PETERSBURG, TWO HUNDRED FREE NEGROES OFFERED FOR ANY WORK THAT MIGHT BE ASSIGNED TO THEM, EITHER TO FIGHT UNDER WHITE OFFICERS, DIG DITCHES, OR ANYTHING THAT COULD SHOW THEIR DESIRE TO SERVE OLD VIRGINIA."

Richmond, Dispatch April 1861

> "I HAVE BUT ONE REGRET I SHALL NOT SOON BE ABLE TO GET AT THE ENEMY."
>
> *Private John Sloan, 9th Texas Infantry, CSA, aged 13*

Rendezvous points like this western Virginia community first saw the gatherings of the clerks and students and farm boys who came to be soldiers. Their rusticity shows in their clothing, soon to be exchanged for Union blue.

The fresh face of this drummer for the Union shows the innocence and touching youth that he will soon lose to the war.

Regardless of their age, background, or even color, those boys who in the spring of 1861, went off to war, saw almost the same sights, felt the same emotions, and shared the same sense of pride and anticipation. It all somehow seemed like a picnic. By land or steamboat they left their county seats and went toward the great training camps that would try to turn them into soldiers. At every stop crowds gathered to cheer them on. Women waved handkerchiefs and handed them pies and cake. Children ran after them, and some thought even the dogs in the street barked in time to the martial music. Philanthropists had meals awaiting them, while some

The drums beat the cadence to which they marched, awoke, ate, and went into battle. These are regimental drums of the Union army. Confederate instruments were far plainer.
Artifacts courtesy of: The Civil War Library and Museum, Philadelphia, Pa.

Yankee recruits encamped in Independence Square, Philadelphia, await the order that will send them off to war, together with all their trappings of soldiering. The image was taken in the summer of 1861; soon encampments like this will seem a luxury.

volunteers traveled with their own cooks, even their own equipment. One New York group brought velvet footstools, leading some to wonder just what kind of war *they* were expecting.

None of them knew what to expect, in reality. Ahead of them lay rude awakenings, hardships and dangers aplenty, and the harsh realization that a war supposed to last only a brief summer was going to drag on for years.

The cap of a Chasseur, one of the fancy regiments like the Zouaves, trained for rapid and intricate drill and movement on the field.
Artifact courtesy of: C. Paul Loane Collection.

CHAPTER TWO

From civilians to soldiers

By long-held custom among American volunteers, the men in the ranks chose their company officers – lieutenants and captains – and then those officers elected the regimental colonel and the other field officers – lieutenant colonel and major. Often as not, the men simply elected the men responsible for raising the regiment, but there were times when ambitious men bought or bullied votes. In the 3d North Carolina Infantry, one lieutenant told a sergeant to have the company fall in. 'Men,' he then addressed them, 'there are two candidates for office, and there is but one of them worth a damn, and I nominate him. All who are in favor of electing Sergeant ------- come to shoulder arms.' That said, the lieutenant ordered, 'company, shoulder arms!' By obeying his order the men cast their votes, unanimously, and without choice. It was not quite democracy in action.

Splendid officers in one of the forts outside Washington display the finery that made officers on both sides seem so dashing, if not overdressed.

The insignia of rank. Shoulder straps displayed an officer's standing, the lowest being the second lieutenant at left, followed by the single bar of the first lieutenant at right.
Artifacts courtesy of: The Civil War Library and Museum, Philadelphia, Pa.

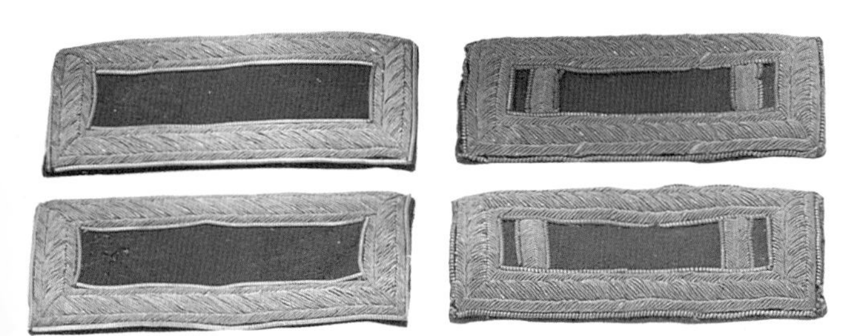

"In the evening Col. Cumming meets us in our barracks and tells us that . . . an election was only a matter of *form* (!) then put it to us by *word of mouth*, whether or not we would sustain him, and no one *daring* to object, he was sustained – This is called an election! What a farce!"

Sergeant Henry A. Buck, Illinois volunteer

Another Chasseur's cap, this one showing the regimental insignia of a unit from one of the big states, New York, Ohio, or Pennsylvania.
Artifacts courtesy of: C. Paul Loane Collection.

Men of the 7th New York, in their gray uniforms, look splendid in 1861. It was up to men like these to select the officers who would lead them to victory or defeat.

No unit in either side's army could match the splendid Zouaves for flashy uniforms, from the turbans and fezzes on their heads, to their baggy pants and white leggings.

A Zouave could come in many variations. This one's cap is almost regulation but for its color, his pants are baggy but not striped like many, and his jacket is unlike any other.

"IN THIS ARMY ONE HOLE IN THE SEAT OF THE BREECHES INDICATES A CAPTAIN, TWO HOLES A LIEUTENANT, AND THE SEAT OF THE PANTS ALL OUT INDICATES THAT THE INDIVIDUAL IS A PRIVATE."

Private Sebron Sneed, Texas Infantry, CSA

Just a few of the Zouave articles include tasseled caps, short coattees with colorful "frogging" or trim, gaiters for the legs, pantaloons, and even a French infantry bugle.
Artifacts courtesy of: Don Troiani Collection.

Barely did he choose – or think he had chosen – his leaders, before the volunteer had his first encounter with government issue bureaucracy – his uniform. In the South, men often simply provided their own, with rough attempts to approximate regulation colors. In practice, Confederates appeared in the field in every color of the rainbow, and sometimes several of them at once. Many wore blue, some even green, and a complete suit of regulation gray was the exception rather than the rule.

In the Union, by contrast, a high degree of uniformity prevailed except among special units like the Zouaves, fancy units outfitted in baggy pantaloons, short jackets, sashes, and fezzes, in the French–Algerian fashion. North and South, a good fit was a dream. Uniforms came in no more than four sizes, and almost everyone got one much too large. One Illinois man completely disappeared inside his suit, with only his ears showing to prove the clothes were inhabited. Only time, adaptation, and water shrinkage, made an eventual fit.

> "THE FIRST THING IN THE MORNING IS DRILL, THEN DRILL, THEN DRILL AGAIN. THEN DRILL, DRILL, A LITTLE MORE DRILL. THEN DRILL, AND LASTLY DRILL. BETWEEN DRILLS, WE DRILL AND SOMETIMES STOP TO EAT A LITTLE AND HAVE ROLL-CALL."
>
> *Oliver Norton, 83d Pennsylvania Infantry*

A selection of the drill manuals officers used to train their volunteers. This group includes special books for infantry, artillery, and cavalry.
Artifacts courtesy of: The Civil War Library and Museum, Philadelphia, Pa., and C. Paul Loane Collection.

In his first weeks in camp, the soldier North or South lived with fife and drum and stentorian sergeants' bawled orders constantly in his ears. Bugles woke him at 5 a.m., sergeants shouted him out onto the parade ground, and then for most of the morning and afternoon he marched and marched and marched. Men with little more grasp of the rudiments of drill than those they now commanded, crammed themselves at night with the rules and

techniques in *Hardee's Tactics* or Silas Casey's *Infantry Tactics*, and then the next day tried to instill it in the men.

It usually started in a shambles. Some backwoods boys barely knew left foot from right, and getting them through the evolutions of company, battalion, regimental, and brigade drill, called for the patience of a saint. Yet it was learning to move quickly and precisely that could make men effective in battle, and which offered them their best protection against a determined enemy.

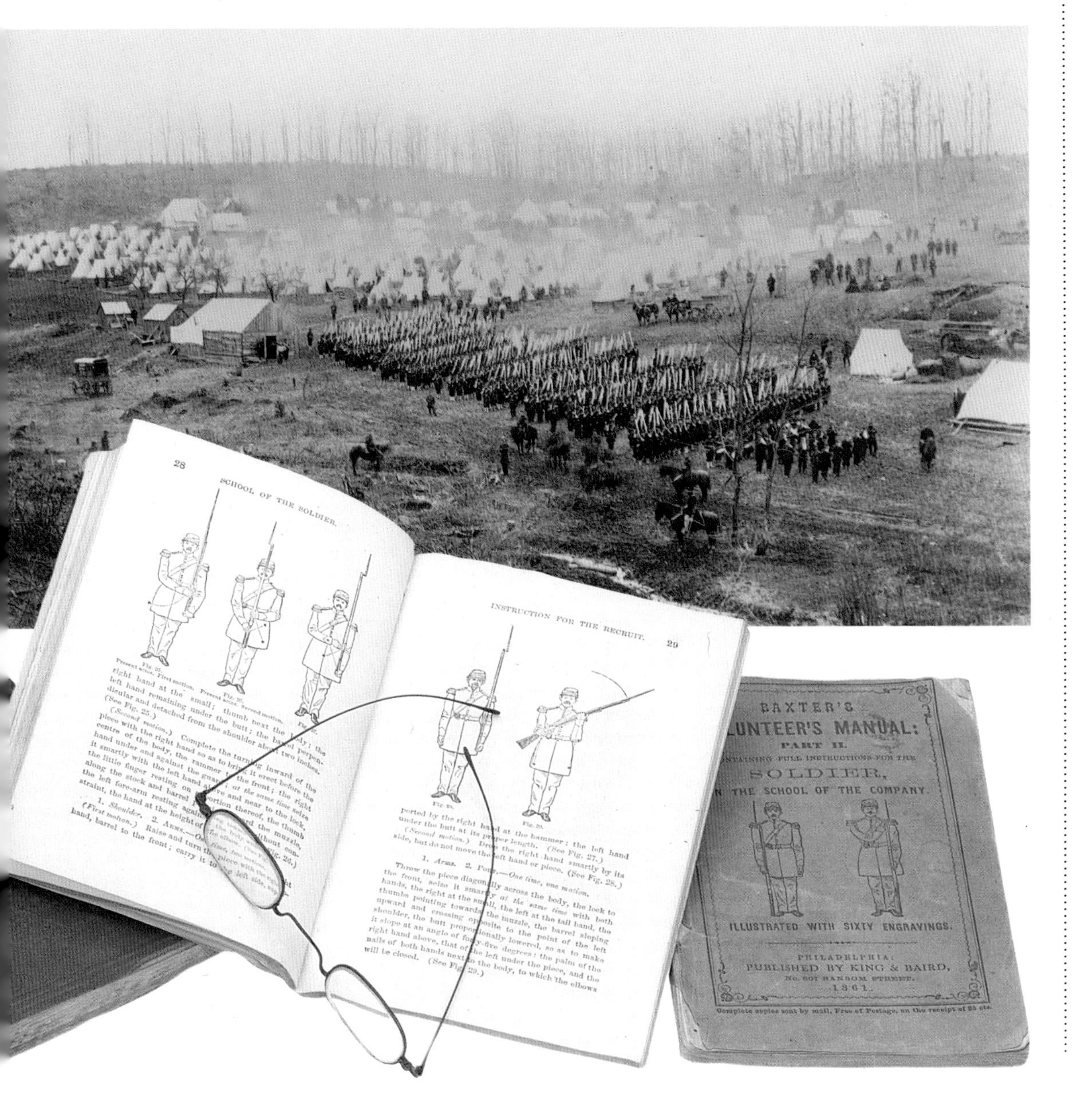

Below left: A New Hampshire regiment practicing at regimental drill in 1862. Making these volunteers think and act in unison called for every ounce of ingenuity and persuasion from their officers.

This anonymous Yankee private looks rather too small for his uniform, and perhaps barely smart enough to learn his drill. Yet of such men did North and South forge great fighting armies.

> “**I** WENT TO THE CONERSARY TO DRAW SOME VISIONS AND SEEIN’ THESE TATERS I CONSECATED THEM.
>
> *Private in the 6th Kentucky Infantry, CSA*

However much they might look like soldiers, Johnny Reb and Billy Yank were always at heart volunteers, with little patience or understanding for army ways.

The common soldier – those who could write – poured out his daily experiences, including his universal frustration with things military – into his diaries and his letters home.
Artifacts courtesy of: The Museum of the Confederacy, Richmond, Va.

There were dozens of bugle calls and special drum beats that the soldier had to memorize, in order to be moved about the battlefield efficiently. Musicians on a battlefield had more than a decorative function.

One of the pitfalls facing new volunteers and their equally new officers was the language of the military. It seemed to differ from English. Now they had to learn words like 'enfilade' and 'echelon,' 'perpendicular,' and more. The Kentucky private who went to the 'commissary' to draw some 'provisions,' and 'confiscated' some potatoes while there, at least did not fumble his words under fire. But these men had to recognize and act on unfamiliar new words quickly, at risk of their lives.

They were never entirely successful. Asked how he would move his outfit to meet a foe on his right front, Lieutenant Nat Clayton of the 4th Kentucky, CSA, replied that, 'I would move the reegi*ment* stauchendiciler to the front.' A fellow Kentucky officer confessed that he could not remember the right commands to give but 'would risk myself and the Trigg County boys, and go in on main strength and awkwardness.' Officers tied bundles of hay and straw to men's feet and taught them left from right by chanting 'hay foot, straw foot' as they marched.

Young Confederates held their equipment belts together with belt plates like these from Maryland at top, Alabama in the center, and Virginia at bottom. *Artifacts courtesy of: Virginia Historical Society, Richmond, Va.*

"THE OFFICERS AND MEN ALL BEING RAW RECRUITS, DISCIPLINE WAS VERY GALLING TO THEM, AND AS THEY WOULD BE BROUGHT UNDER RIGID MILITARY DISCIPLINE A LARGE AMOUNT OF FIRST-CLASS SWEARING COULD BE HEARD EVERY DAY; BUT SOON THE BOYS BEGAN TO LEARN THE 'OLD SOLDIER' TRICKS AND LEARNED TO YIELD GRACEFULLY TO THE INEVITABLE WHEN THEY COULD NOT DODGE THE OFFICERS."

James R. Binford, 15th Mississippi Infantry

Three Confederate soldiers, all from the same regiment, wear three different hats with their uniforms, evidence that regulations were honored mostly in the breach thanks to shortages.

A tattered Palmetto flag once carried by a South Carolina regiment, and displaying their crudely fashioned fighting motto: "OUR RIGHTS WE DEFEND."
Artifact courtesy of: The Museum of the Confederacy, Richmond, Va.

Union soldiers west of the Appalachians rest around their stacked arms, the day's drill behind them.

The object of all the drill was only partly to move the men about the field. It was also to train them to obey instantly and without question, something that these volunteers would never do entirely willingly. North and South, they came to fight, not to parade, and even after four years of war, many a Reb and Yank still did not see the use of discipline, nor feel the least inclined to yield any of his prized personal independence. Blind obedience simply did not dwell within him.

'I love my country as well as any one,' said a Georgia boy, 'but I don't believe in the plan of making myself a slave.' None of them did, and it is not mere hyperbole that led their officers and others since to claim them to be the best fighters and the worst *soldiers* America has ever borne.

Just a few of the many experimental breachloading weapons tried during the war, including at top the Burnside carbine, invented by General Ambrose Burnside, the very effective 7-shot Spencer repeating carbine, and at bottom the less successful Smith carbine.
Artifacts courtesy of: The Civil War Library and Museum, Philadelphia, Pa.

Part of the drill and discipline was to prepare the volunteers for handling the deadly weapons entrusted to them. Infantrymen got muskets or rifles, with bayonets, while a cavalryman got a carbine, usually a pistol, and a saber as well. All could and did kill, and were as deadly to friend as foe if not properly used.

"IF OUR MEN SHOOT AT THE ENEMY LIKE THEY DID AT THAT BARREL, THEY WILL NOT KILL VERY MANY OF THE ENEMY UNLESS THEY CLIMB LIKE SQUIRRELS OR GET IN THE GROUND LIKE MOLES; FOR THOSE THAT DID NOT HIT THE TREE TOP HIT THE GROUND ABOUT HALF WAY TO THE TARGET."

Jesse W. Reid, 4th South Carolina Infantry, CSA

The edged weapons soon proved next to useless. Horsemen usually did more damage to themselves and their animals with their swords than to any enemy, while foot soldiers soon found the best use for their bayonets to be as candle sticks and meat spits. In the whole war they inflicted less than half of one percent of all wounds.

It was the firearms, and especially the rifles, that took the toll, and then thanks chiefly to volume of fire rather than accuracy. Reb and Yank never became any better marksmen than they were soldiers.

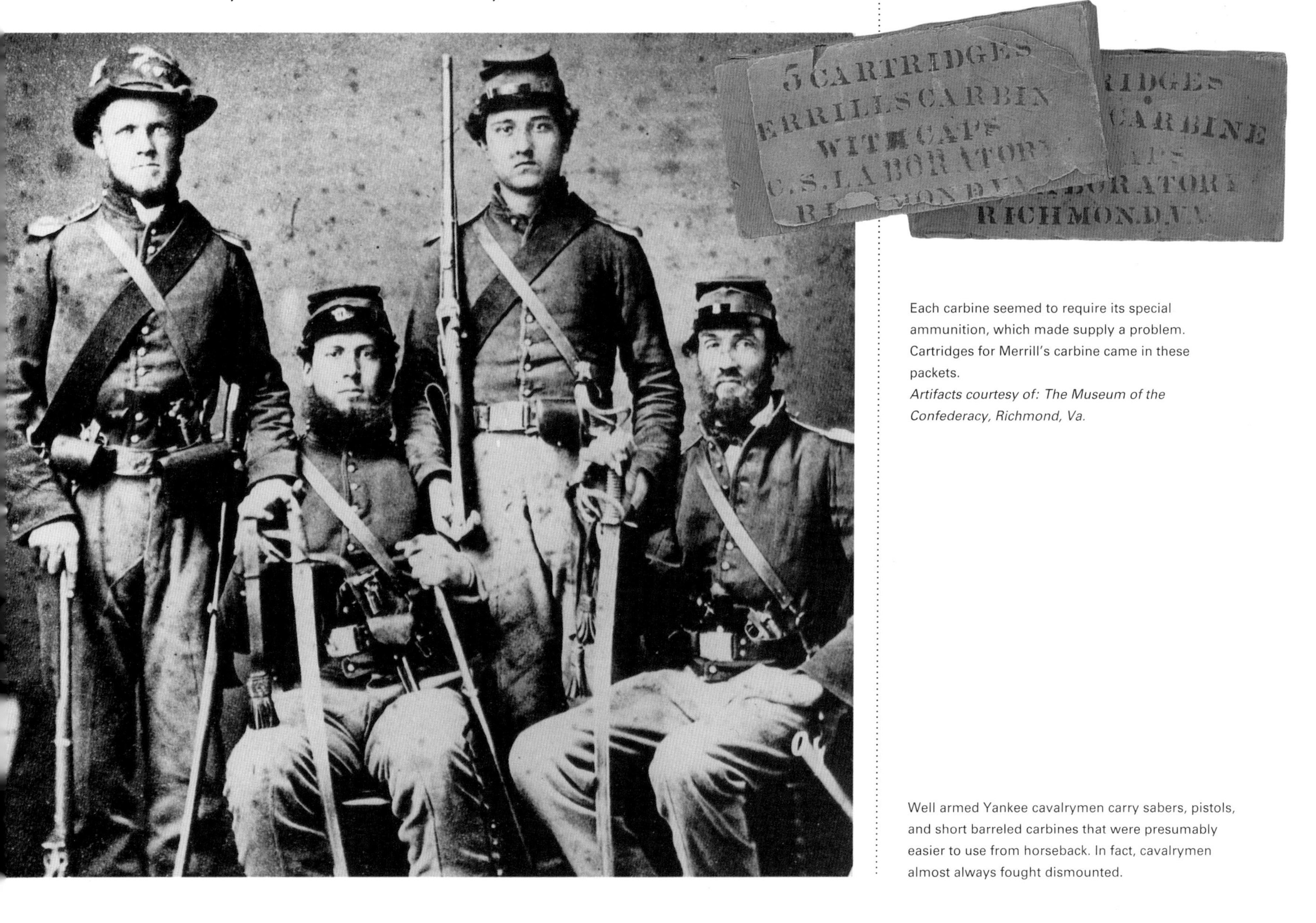

Each carbine seemed to require its special ammunition, which made supply a problem. Cartridges for Merrill's carbine came in these packets.
Artifacts courtesy of: The Museum of the Confederacy, Richmond, Va.

Well armed Yankee cavalrymen carry sabers, pistols, and short barreled carbines that were presumably easier to use from horseback. In fact, cavalrymen almost always fought dismounted.

The exhaustingly full day of the new volunteer also served to keep him too busy to fall prey to every soldier's enemy, homesickness. It could, quite literally, kill. Those in its clutches fell into despondency, lost appetite, and thus weakened in constitution were easy prey for other camp diseases. Every letter from home only made more stark the difference between sleeping in a rude tent surrounded by strangers, and being at home amid the friends and relatives of a lifetime. Word of some tragedy at home made the miles of separation seem longer. Glad tidings made more cruel the fact that the soldiers missed the happy event. 'More men die of homesickness than all other diseases,' one Iowa man claimed with some exaggeration, 'and when a man gives up and lies down he is a *goner*.'

A soldier fought homesickness as he could. Carrying these images of his loved ones made him feel at least a little closer to the people in the images. *Artifacts courtesy of: The Museum of the Confederacy, Richmond, Va.*

Most men kept in touch with home and hearth as did this soldier of the Confederate 5th Georgia, by writing letters.

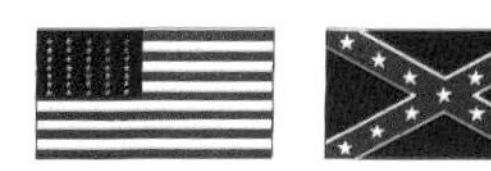

Just a sampling of the literally millions of soldier letters written during the war, many of them on patriotic stationery proclaiming confidence in country and cause.
Artifacts courtesy of: The Civil War Library and Museum, Philadelphia, Pa.

"IF I HAD BEEN SUDDENLY THROWN FROM THE COMFORTS OF HOME, AND THE SCENES OF PROSPERITY AROUND ME INTO SUCH A PLACE AS THIS I SHOULD HAVE THOUGHT IT HORRIBLE, VERY HORRIBLE, BUT WE HAVE BECOME USED TO IT, WE ARE AS CHEERFUL AND HAPPY AS YOU ARE; ONLY WHEN WE THINK OF HOME, THEN OH HOW OUR HEARTS SICKEN."

Alfred L. Hough, Pennsylvania Infantry, USA

"CHRISTOPHER DIMICK WAS DED THAT MAKES 3 OF THE DOVER BOYS THAT HAS DIED OUT OF 42 AND ONE KILLED. THAT IS ABOUT THE WAY THERE IS MORE DIES BY SICKNESS THAN GETS KILLED."

Andrew K. Rose, Ohio Infantry, USA

A soldier's nightmare was being wounded and coming under the 'care' of the surgeon, who no matter how conscientious, was still groping blindly in search of healing. All too often his only weapon against infection and death was the scalpel and the saw.
Artifacts courtesy of: The Museum of the Confederacy, Richmond, Va.

Private Rose was closer to the truth than he knew. More than 600,000 men died in the war, and more than three-fourths of them succumbed to disease. Suddenly in 1861 boys and men who had lived isolated lives and never been exposed to large numbers of people, were thrown into the company of tens of thousands. Simple childhood diseases like measles and chicken pox ravaged through the camps. Measles alone killed tens of thousands. Worse, doctors 'examined' and passed untold numbers of men too ill to serve, who then went on to infect others. And on top of that, there were no medicines other than purgatives, no anaesthetics other than ether and opiates, and not even a concept of sanitation.

As a result, the war was a carnival for microbes. Simple wounds became gangrenous, resulting in amputation or death. A white soldier could expect to be sick at least two and one-half times a year, and a black soldier three and one-half times. A bullet would kill six soldiers out of 100. Disease would claim more than sixteen.

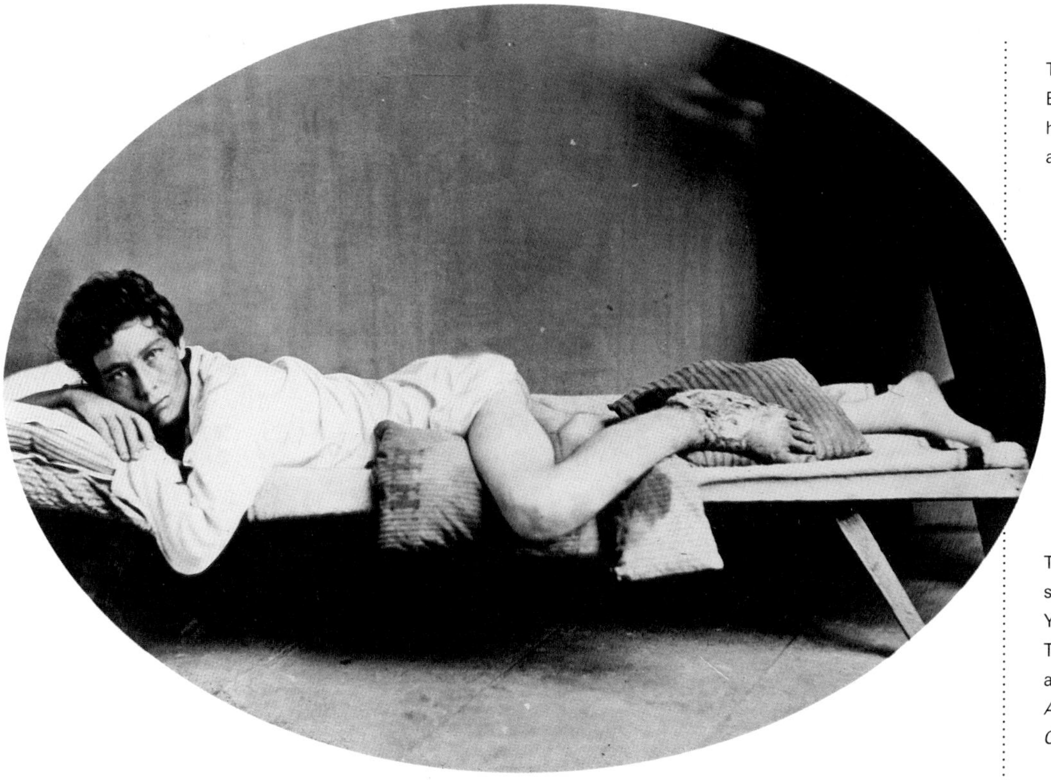

This soldier's misery started as an injury to the ankle. But gangrene has set in, the foot had become hideously disfigured and infected, and it will be amputated.

The uniform and instruments of the Confederate surgeon. He was nearly as well equipped as his Yankee counterpart, except for medications. Thankfully, there was usually enough opiate anaesthetic for his "operations."
Artifacts courtesy of: The Museum of the Confederacy, Richmond, Va.

CHAPTER THREE

Life in camp

In the soldier's monotonous life, no time was more important than meals. These are the items that he used to prepare and eat his food, from the conical Sibley stove, to the coffee boiler and mess kits. The plate holds a piece of hardtack.
Artifacts courtesy of: The Museum of the Confederacy, Richmond, Va.

The recruits went to the armies besotted with the idea that being a soldier would be nothing but fighting and glory. They had no notion of such a thing as camping half a year at a time on some muddy or frozen plain, occupied with nothing more than marching and countermarching. Moreover, no one taught them to cook, or pitch tents, or not to dig their latrines upstream of their camps.

Most of all, no one taught them how to handle the incalculable hours they found on their hands after those initial weeks of drill were done, and

For every hour in battle, the soldier spent weeks – even months – in routine camp chores, cutting wood, washing clothes, and more. A fortunate few had wives who followed the armies and helped.

when they were not actually on campaign. It was a seemingly endless routine of awake, clean camp, eat, drill and detail work, another meal, mending uniforms, cleaning weapons, and always an incessant talk of battles won and lost, of home and family, and of hope for the future.

> "LET US TOGETHER RECALL WITH PLEASURE THE PAST! ONCE MORE BE HUNGRY, AND EAT; ONCE MORE TIRED, AND REST; ONCE MORE THIRSTY, AND DRINK; ONCE MORE COLD AND WET, LET US SIT BY THE ROARING FIRE AND FEEL COMFORT CREEP OVER US."
>
> *Carlton McCarthy, Richmond Howitzers, CSA*

> "IN COLD OR RAINY WEATHER, WHEN EVERY OPENING IS CLOSED, THEY ARE MOST UNWHOLESOME TENEMENTS, AND TO ENTER ONE OF THEM OF A RAINY MORNING FROM THE OUTER AIR, AND ENCOUNTER THE NIGHT'S ACCUMULATION OF NAUSEATING EXHALATIONS FROM THE BODIES OF TWELVE MEN (DIFFERING WIDELY IN THEIR HABITS OF PERSONAL CLEANLINESS) WAS AN EXPERIENCE WHICH NO OLD SOLDIER HAS EVER BEEN KNOWN TO RECALL WITH ANY GREAT ENTHUSIASM."
>
> *John D. Billings, 10th Massachusetts Artillery, USA*

The proud pennant of a Yankee regiment that saw action in every major battle in the East. The emblem in the center is that of the 5th Corps, Army of the Potomac.

A large Union winter quarters in Virginia shows the substantial huts and houses built by some regiments. Virtual log cities, with named streets and even sidewalks, sometimes appeared in the countryside. The soldiers could be living there for months.

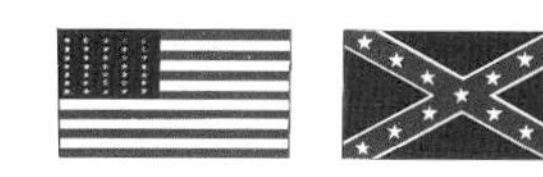

Around the ruins of a burned house, soldiers have erected their shelters and temporary stockade as the army passes by.

Not surprisingly, shelter was very important to the soldier, even if it was a stinking Sibley tent like the one Billings described. In summer and fall a tent was his only protection from rain and sun, and winter and spring the log and canvas 'houses' built for winter quarters kept out *some* of the icy blasts.

Tents came in every shape, from the two-man 'dog' tent, to huge 'wall' tents that accommodated up to twenty. Most were cumbersome to handle, and afforded at best minimal comfort. The more imaginative and substantial winter housing, on the other hand, could include fireplaces, and even board floors. Even then, soldiers showed their attitude toward their shelter by dubbing their dwellings 'Swine Hotel,' 'Starvation Alley,' and 'Mud Lane.'

The high crowned Hardee hat, with the insignia of the engineers, overlooks a forage kepi marked with a regiment's number and company letter.

The soldier who expected his army rations to provide any diversion from monotony was soon disappointed. His meat came either salted, pickled, or so freshly killed that he could still taste the blood in it. Even the preserved meat was sometimes so spoiled it looked 'blue' and would stick like glue when thrown against a tree.

Bread could be baked fresh daily when in winter camp, but on the march the men ate 'army bread,' a tough, tooth-cracking cracker called hardtack, but more often known as 'sheet-iron crackers,' 'tooth dullers,' and 'worm castles' thanks to their being inhabited by maggots. Vegetables, when they got them, came raw from the fields, or 'dessicated' – dehydrated – and pressed into cakes.

Hardly any of it was nourishing, and much of it was disgusting. Soldiers held mock funerals for their beef rations, claimed mystical properties for the rock-hard crackers, and undermined their health by frying all of it in a sea of grease.

Whenever the army stopped in one place long enough, the commissaries began baking fresh bread to supplement the hardtack issue. Amongst the filth of camp, dough rises in pans in the sun, while a baker kneads more in the trough.

A soldier tends a meal frying in the ubiquitous grease over a small portable tin stove, while comrades in the "winterized" Sibley tents do the same.

Cooking utensils were usually little more than a skillet and a few bowls, with dinner ware inevitably of tin. Many soldiers carried combination cutlery of the type seen here.
Artifacts courtesy of: The Civil War Library and Museum, Philadelphia, Pa., and J. Craig Nannos Collection.

"YESTERDAY MORNING WAS THE FIRST TIME WE HAD TO CARRY OUR MEAT FOR THE MAGGOTS ALWAYS CARRIED IT TILL THEN. WE HAD TO HAVE AN EXTRA GARD TO KEEP THEM FROM PACKING IT CLEAR OFF."

Charles Anderson, Ohio Infantry, USA

Not only camp cooking worked against the health of the soldier when not on campaign. He dug his latrines in the wrong places, and then often as not just answered nature's call wherever he felt like it, even outside the flap of his tent. Camp garbage, and especially the carcasses of butchered livestock, attracted legions of flies. Required by regulations to bathe once a week, many soldiers never washed for the entire war excepting dunkings when they crossed streams on the march.

Then there were the vermin. Fleas, lice, flies, mosquitoes, and more, banqueted on Johnny Reb and Billy Yank. Calling lice 'graybacks,' the soldiers made a sport of hunting them in each other's hair and clothing, and some swore that dead lice were found with the letters 'I.F.W.' – 'In For the War' on their backs. Another soldier tried killing them, 'but as I believe 40 of them comes to every one's funeral, I have given it up as a bad job.'

Concepts of cleanliness were lax in the extreme, and sanitation barely existed in the camps. With time on their hands in winter huts like these, men washed their clothing more often, but they could never rid themselves of the ever-present lice.

Many a soldier rarely if ever bathed himself, and when he did it was usually in temperate weather when a convenient stream offered a cooling dip.

"I HAVE SEEN MEN LITERALLY WEAR OUT THEIR UNDERCLOTHES WITHOUT A CHANGE AND WHEN THEY THREW THEM OFF THEY WOULD SWARM WITH VERMIN LIKE A LIVE ANT HILL WHEN DISTURBED."

Cyrus F. Boyd, 15th Iowa Infantry, USA

Men who neglected the basics of cleanliness sooner or later had need of the surgeon.
Artifacts courtesy of: The Museum of the Confederacy, Richmond, Va.

"MANY OF THE MEN HAD NOT BEEN MUCH FROM HOME, AND TO SAY THAT THEY WERE HOMESICK IS TO STATE THE FACT VERY MILDLY. OTHERS, THROWING OFF THE RESTRAINTS OF HOME, ACTED MORE LIKE WILD COLTS THAN ANYTHING ELSE. A VERY LARGE MAJORITY WERE, HOWEVER, STEADY, EARNEST MEN, AS RELIABLE IN CAMP AS OUT OF IT."

L. W. Day, 101st Ohio Infantry, USA

For entertainment, the soldiers looked to every pastime imaginable, though in a musical era when everyone sang, they most often took pleasure in the sound of regimental bands and informal ensembles. Songs of home were always welcome.

Never did American men find their ingenuity as challenged as when presented with spending the greater part of four years in idleness. Those who could, wrote incessantly, diaries for themselves, and letters to send home to family, friends, even the local newspapers. Those who could read, did, and some regiments even established small libraries, and anything in print could pass the time. When not reading, they sang and played the instruments available, usually guitar, fiddle, or banjo. 'All Quiet Along the Potomac,' they sang, or 'The Vacant Chair,' melodies reflecting their melancholy at absence from home. But stirring marches also issued from the tents, as well as hymns.

They formed debating societies and glee clubs, put on plays, teased and played practical jokes, had snowball fights in winter, and staged athletic contests in summer. Most of all, they just talked.

Idle hours were filled with every manner of occupation – watercolors, chess, cards, reading and writing, carving animal horns, playing the guitar or flute, molding bullets, and more.
Artifacts courtesy of: The Museum of the Confederacy, Richmond, Va.

Despite the best efforts of officers opposed to gambling, cards and dice were to be found in almost every tent in the armies North and South. So fond of cards were the soldiers that they often posed for photographers, cards in hand.

"WHILE ALMOST IRREPRESSIBLY FOND OF WHISKY, AND INCORRIGIBLE WHEN NOT ON ACTIVE SERVICE, ABOUT STRAGGLING THROUGH THE COUNTRY AND RUNNING OUT OF CAMP, THEY . . . ARE ALWAYS BEHAVING BADLY."

General Basil W. Duke, CSA

What General Duke said about Kentucky Confederates applied to all soldiers. They were always up to something, and much of it defied regulations.

Some pastimes were relatively benign. Pornographic photographs and racy novels were popular, if banned in the camps. Profanity, of course, was epidemic. But this was mild compared to the gambling. Soldiers bet on everything from dice to cards to hog races. All too often the losers turned to theft, and if a loser at cards did not steal to recoup his losses, he often as not challenged the winner to a fight. Brawling relieved tension, of which there was always too much. On one memorable occasion, the 7th Missouri had 900 fights in a single day.

Most misbehavior could be traced in the end to drinking, which was epidemic when liquor was available. Prostitution brought venereal disease into camp as well, and a combination of all these things – or being denied them – led to insubordination toward those in authority that even the best officers could never completely eradicate.

A soldier's haversack could yield all sorts of entertainments, but usually a deck of cards, a diary, perhaps a book or two, and everyday articles like a homemade razor and combination cutlery. *Artifacts courtesy of: The Museum of the Confederacy, Richmond, Va.*

'If there is any place on God's fair earth where wickedness "stalketh abroad in daylight," it is in the army,' complained an Illinois soldier. No one needed to tell that to the chaplains who tried to bring spiritual comfort and support to the men in the ranks. Catholic, Protestant, or Jew, they all tried to hang on to the faithful, and bring more to the faith, saving them from the sinfulness that beckoned in idle hours.

In fact, most soldiers went to war with some religious background, and despite the horrors they saw on the battlefield, few actually lost their faith, though most relaxed their behavior. The Bible was the most commonly seen book in camp, and Sunday services were usually well attended, especially when battle was imminent. In 1864 in the Confederacy, a major revival swept the armies as in the darkest days of the conflict men sought success in renewed faith. Theirs was a simple faith, North and South, that looked to an all-powerful Almighty to grant them victory.

Along with their cards and their sometimes sinful ways, Rebs and Yanks took their religion to war with them. Here the priest of an Irish regiment conducts a mass, but every denomination known was represented in the armies.

> "THE LARGE PROPORTION OF THE SOLDIERS WERE WICKED AND MANY WERE RECKLESS. FOR MORE THAN A YEAR VERY FEW MANIFESTED ANY DESIRE TO BECOME CHRISTIANS SAVE THE SICK OR WOUNDED."
>
> *J. William Jones, Chaplain, CSA*

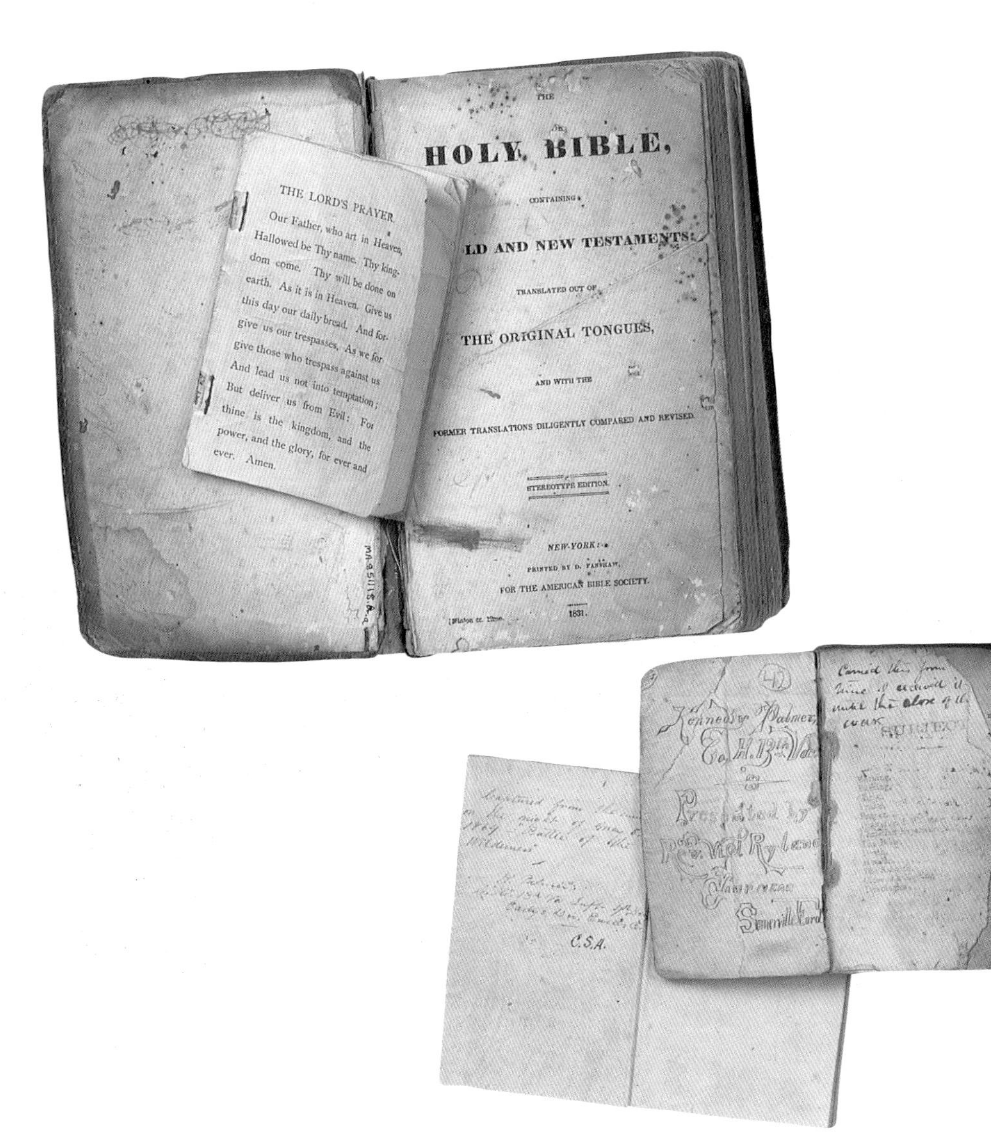

The American Bible Society distributed tens of thousands of bibles like this in the Union armies, along with pamphlets of the Lord's Prayer. Soldiers often carried small prayer books with them into battle.

Artifacts courtesy of: The Museum of the Confederacy, Richmond, Va.

> "AFTER SUPPER THE MEN GATHERED AROUND THE FIRES FOR A SMOKE AND TO LISTEN TO THE GOSSIP OF THE REGIMENT. IT FREQUENTLY HAPPENS THAT SOMEONE WILL INVENT A STORY, REQUESTING THE STRICTEST SECRECY, IN ORDER THAT IT MAY TRAVEL THE FASTER."
>
> *Charles E. Davis, 13th Massachusetts Infantry, USA*

News in wartime is always a precious commodity. If the enlisted men had to rely on rumor for his information, his senior officers were far better served. The electric telegraph, like these Confederate examples below, helped the commanders and politicians of both sides keep control of a war being fought on a continental scale.
Artifacts courtesy of: The Museum of the Confederacy, Richmond, Va.

As time went on, army discipline and the experience of war forged regiments into tight-knit units, bound together by a comradeship which gave an edge to camp life and the inevitable regimental gossip.

If he survived the war and made it home, some of the veteran's most distinctive memories would be of life in camp and the hours spent in conversation.

When all was said and done, after gambling and drinking and pranking and praying, the most popular single pastime for soldiers of both armies was simply talking. Politics, philosophy, reminiscences, the progress of the war, any topic could draw a conversation to pass an afternoon or evening. Mostly they speculated on the campaigns to come, the prospects for peace, when they would be home again, and what it would be like. 'I never heard so many lies in my life as are told in camp,' complained one boy, and even the most imaginative rumors enjoyed only short lives, while those who told them were soon spotted as liars.

But it was the talking that most safely vented their frustrations and fears, and it was here, too, that their irrepressible humor came out best, even if in fantastic tales punctuated by colorful language, some of it invented. 'I was squashmolished,' one soldier said of a mishap, but everyone knew what he meant. It was part of the growing language of the camps.

CHAPTER FOUR

The leaders and the led

With the exception of the pitiful few hundred Old Army officers available in 1861, no one North or South knew or understood command. All of the volunteer officers had to learn it, and the experience came hard to many. There were no schools to teach them. Frantically they read the latest drill manuals, sometimes writing the orders on slips of paper, then reading them at practice the next day – hoping the wind did not blow them away. Inevitably they gave orders out of sequence, confusing themselves and their equally inexperienced troops. 'That the men got into a snarl, a tangle, a double and twisted, inextricable tactical knot, is tame delineation,' confessed one. 'The drill caused a great deal of serious reflection.'

Then there was learning to do the paperwork, filing forms to get the men fed, clothed, and paid. In the end, only experience, trial and error, turned men into leaders, and revealed those who were not.

Outside Petersburg in 1865, Pennsylvanian volunteers rest while their officers await further orders.

Published at the very beginning of the war, the Confederacy's book of dress regulations for its officers set a standard that men in the field were seldom able to achieve.
Artifacts courtesy of: The Museum of the Confederacy, Richmond, Va.

"MY POST IS NO SINECURE. MY HANDS ARE FULL – PERFECTLY FULL. I HAVE NO HOPE OF BEING A POPULAR CAPT. I AM ONLY TRYING TO MAKE A GOOD ONE. NO ONE CAN IMAGINE THE AMT. OF WORK REQUIRED OF AN OFFICER AS GREEN AS I AM IN TACTICS."

A Mississippi captain of infantry, CSA

The regimental colors of the 18th US Infantry.

> "I WISH TO GOD ONE HALF OF OUR OFFICERS WERE KNOCKED IN THE HEAD BY SLINGING THEM AGAINST A PART OF THOSE STILL LEFT."
>
> *A Yankee private*

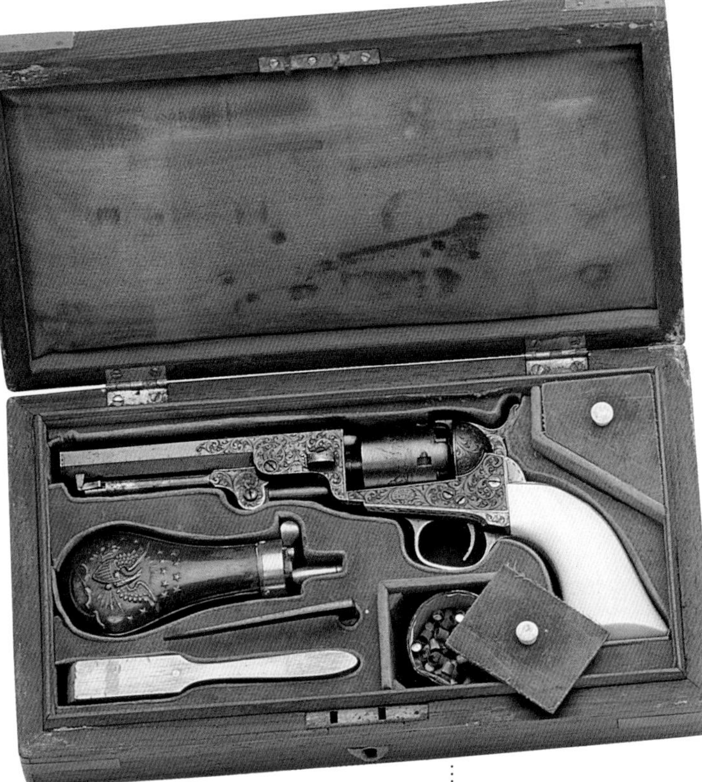

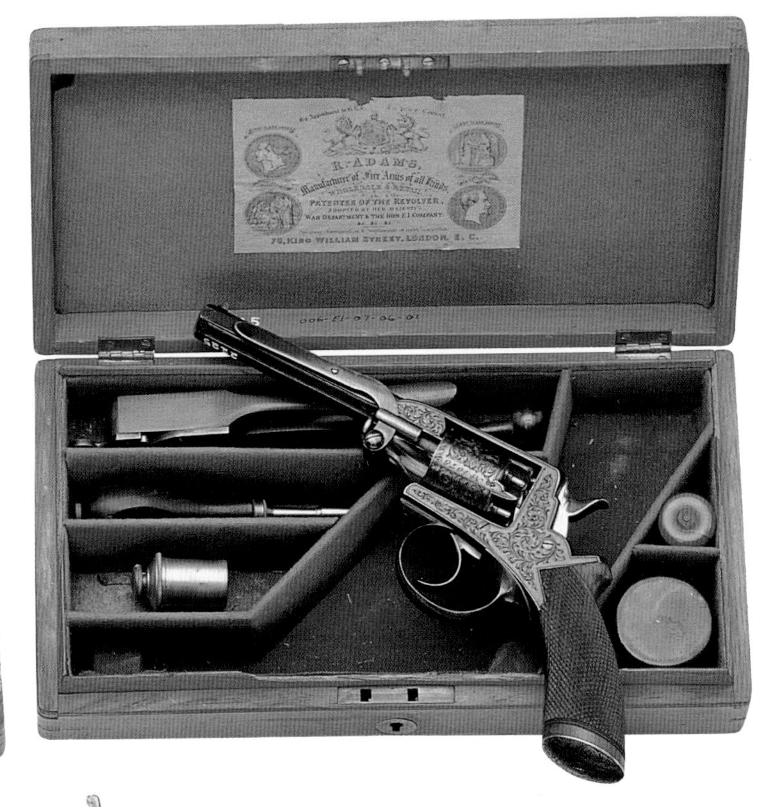

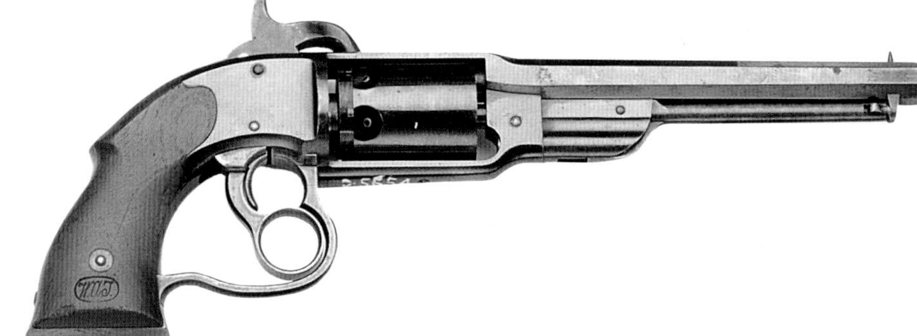

Fancy engraved pistols in presentation cases were strictly the province of the officers, from the Colt "Navy" .36 at left, to the more exotic Adams import next to it. Very few, however, carried something like the Savage-North .36, below right.
Artifacts courtesy of: West Point Museum, West Point, NY.

Some men chosen to command simply never measured up to the task. Many could not take the pressure of their new job, the disapproval of the men, or the contempt of other, better officers. Others found themselves repelled by the dirt and squalor, and the crudeness of army life, not to mention the company they had to keep. One Texan described a major who gave up his commission, saying that 'if he had to associate with devils, he would wait till he went to hell, where he could select his own company.'

Some unfit officers stayed with the armies, doing irreparable harm. Cowardice, drunkenness, and neglect, made their men suffer unnecessarily, and contributed toward poor morale. 'There is a great deal of disatisfaction with the Capt.,' said an Illinois private. 'He [is] so bigoted that he will not learn any thing and he cannot drill half as good as the men and the other commissioned officers are not much better.' When the best officers sometimes had trouble controlling soldiers, bad officers could turn even good men into a bad regiment.

Several officers of the Union's Army of the Potomac pose casually beside a field piece. They, too, observed an indifference to dress that reflected their individuality.

"I think I am under one of the Best Captains in the world."

A soldier of the First Kentucky Brigade, CSA

Colonel Ambrose Burnside as he appeared as commander of the 1st Rhode Island. Looking every inch the soldier, Burnside inspired his men and gained the confidence of politicians in Washington until he rose in rank and failed disastrously as commander of the Army of the Potomac.

For every bad officer in the armies, many good ones emerged. For one thing, the first regiments to join the colors were in for one year enlistments only. When those soldiers re-enlisted for three years or the war, they had learned something about what they needed in commanders, and showed much better judgment in the officers they elected the second time around. Moreover, state governors learned, too, and gave their appointments for field ranks to better qualified men who had already proven themselves.

And of course, experience had been a great teacher. Natural leaders gradually emerged, men like Joshua Chamberlain of the 20th Maine or John B. Gordon of the 6th Alabama, whose men would and did follow them into the cannon's mouth. Such officers looked after their paperwork, which was in effect looking after the men. They led from the front rank, and off the battlefield made the privates' concerns their own. It was no wonder that such officers usually started out as company lieutenants and captains, inevitably found promotion to senior rank, and with it the enduring respect and affection of their men.

The uniform frock coats of a Union first lieutenant, a colonel of the 118th Connecticut, and a colonel of the 169th New York. They show the wide variation in officers' uniforms.
Artifacts courtesy of: The Civil War Library and Museum, Philadelphia, Pa., and Don Troiani Collection.

Officers had the kind of responsibility that could allow them to betray their trusts. Commissaries like the man in charge of this bakery could cheat the men and the army in quality of goods in order to profit personally.

Officers were men and boys, too, and they could abuse their rank and misbehave just as surely as any private, only the man with rank stood a better chance of getting away with it. Their besetting sin was drunkenness. It could extend from merely being inebriated on the drill field, to intoxication on the battlefield. One Yankee officer got himself cashiered when he became so drunk at an officers' mess that he stood on the table and relieved himself on the food. Then, too, gambling lured them, and they had more to wager than their soldiers, nor were they immune to the baser urges served by camp followers. Some officers kept prostitutes with them in their quarters, and even a few generals like Yankees Judson Kilpatrick and Joseph Hooker became notorious for their indiscretions.

Perhaps worst of all were the thieves. As the armies rapidly expanded and their supply requirements soared, so the temptation to make a personal profit from the soldiers' needs grew. Men in charge of army bureaucracy could embezzle, and a few did, most notably General Justus McKinstry, who extorted bribes from contractors supplying goods to the Union army, and was cashiered for his crime.

> "THERE IS A GREAT DEAL OF DISSATISFACTION ABOUT OUR COLONEL THEY DONT LIKE HIM ATALL I HANT GOT NO USE FOR HIM HE IS ALWAYS DRUNK WHEN HE CAN GET WHISKEY."
>
> *John Cotton, 10th Confederate Cavalry*

General Joseph Hooker was famous for his inappropriate conduct with women and drink. He was to resign his army command in 1864.

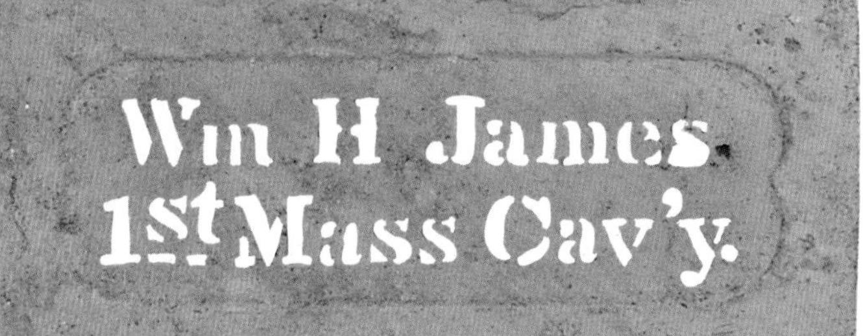

With the dog-tag a thing of the future, men and officers carried stencils and identity discs that they purchased on their own.
Artifacts courtesy of: Wendell Lang Collection, Tarrytown, NY.

> "IF THARE IS ONE THING THAT I HATE MORE THAN ANOTHER IT IS THE SIGHT OF A SHOULDER STRAP, FOR I AM WELL CONVINCED IN MY OWN MIND THAT HAD IT NOT BEEN FOR OFFICERS THIS WAR WOULD HAVE ENDED LONG AGO."
>
> *George Gray Hunter, Pennsylvania soldier*

While the men may have cursed their regimental officers, they rarely had anything but praise for the likes of these men. In pursuit of Lee's Army of Northern Virginia, at a council of war at Massaponax Church in 1864, General U. S. Grant leans over the bench at left studying a map with General George G. Meade, while officers of their staffs look on.

Typical Confederate artillery officers' uniform items. Jackets, shirts, gauntlets, holsters and belts, sabers, binoculars, and more, were the usual effects worn and carried by commanders of the big guns. *Artifacts courtesy of: The Museum of the Confederacy, Richmond, Va., and Russ Pritchard Collection.*

It is rare in any army or any war that the enlisted man does not at one time or another disparage his officers, if for nothing more than the fact that they *are* his officers. Johnny Reb and Billy Yank made it clear early on that they would yield their independence only grudgingly, and award their respect with equal reluctance. Damning their officers became a part of their campfire pastime, and some were remarkably imaginative about it. They applied all manner of epithets to the leaders, from 'bugger' and 'dog,' to 'Greenhorn,' 'skunk,' and 'whorehouse pimp.' But the all-time favorite was the classic 'son of a bitch.'

One soldier declared his colonel 'an ignoramus fit for nothing higher than the cultivation of corn,' while a Reb from Florida pronounced his officers 'not fit to tote guts to a Bear.' So long as they kept those opinions to themselves, the private soldiers had little to fear.

Officers had to be careful of the insubordinate soldier, for among other things he had been trained to kill, and he carried weapons like this sword-bayonet, and the Model 1841 "Mississippi" Rifle above, or the Sharps rifle below.
Artifacts courtesy of: The Civil War Library and Museum, Philadelphia, Pa., and J. Craig Nannos Collection, Philadelphia, Pa.

"YOU ORDER ME! YOU AINT WORTH A PINCH OF SHIT! YOU KISS MY ARSE, YOU GOD DAMNED LOUSE."

An unidentified Union soldier

From time to time there were soldiers who could not keep their resentment of officers under rein. When that happened, trouble was bound to ensue. Insubordination took many forms, and much of it was induced by drinking. Most of all, soldiers simply talked back to their officers or hurled insults at them. 'Shit-house adjutant,' they yelled, or 'old puke,' or 'illiterate ass.'

More active insubordination came in refusing to obey an order, and sometimes that resulted in the most outright rebellion, striking an officer. A punch or a kick, even a shove, was a severe breach of military law, but some soldiers could not restrain themselves. One Yankee threw a heavy iron grapeshot at his colonel, narrowly missing him. A captain who insulted a picket guard found himself pulled from his horse and thoroughly beaten, while an army inspector who threatened some soldiers with his sword was pulled from his mount and severely battered. At the most extreme, a soldier might draw a weapon, rifle or sword, and threaten an officer with it. If he stopped short of striking, he was fortunate, for penalties could be swift and summary.

A typical field quarters for regimental officers showed a little more comfort than that enjoyed by the enlisted ranks, including camp beds, tables, and chairs. The responsibility of command had some compensations.

> "I KILLED HIM. THE COMPANY WANTED HIM KILLED . . . I KILLED THE SON OF A BITCH AND I WAS THE ONLY MAN IN THE COMPANY WHO HAD THE HEART TO DO IT."
>
> *An Illinois sergeant*

The soldier had an array of weapons to try, some experimental like these Ketcham hand grenades. Such weapons were often as dangerous to the user as they were to an enemy.
Artifacts courtesy of: Gettysburg Museum of the Civil War, Gettysburg, Pa.

Occasionally the resentment – often mixed with intemperance – became too much to bear. If an officer were fortunate, the revenge taken on him by aggrieved soldiers came in the form of a cruel joke. Unpopular officers overly fond of their horses could awake one morning to find the animal with shaved mane and clipped tail. Others were locked in the privies or had their tents rifled or booby-trapped to fall down around them in the night.

A few officers experienced the most extreme manifestation of soldier resentment. The Illinois sergeant who testified after killing his captain was not alone. Occasionally men vowed that they had 'spotted' a hated officer,

These are the remnants of a Spencer carbine at top, a Sharps carbine below it, and a Colt .44 Army pistol.
Artifacts courtesy of: Wendell Lang Collection, Tarrytown, NY.

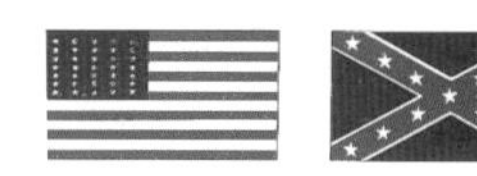

meaning that in the next battle they would kill him if the enemy did not. Men of the 6th New Hampshire tried repeatedly to kill General Thomas Williams in action, but missed him. Confederate General Charles Winder fell to a Yankee shell on the same battlefield where his own men intended to shoot him if they could.

The Dunker Church at Antietam, photographed shortly after the battle, with some of the dead lying near where they fell. These were the grisliest artifacts of all.

For the worst misbehavior, a firing squad could await a soldier like this man, kneeling in prayer against the coffin he will soon inhabit for eternity.

When the soldiers got out of line, the punishments could be anything from a rebuke to a firing squad, and often the penalty did not fit the crime, but rather reflected the caprice of the officers in charge. Some were inordinately lenient, treating even capital offenses with what one Confederate called 'a little fatherly advice'. Others might visit years of imprisonment at hard labor for a minor infraction. The result was that soldiers did not know what to expect, making the threat of punishment a weakened deterrent.

"THERE WAS A CLASS OF OFFICERS WHO FELT THAT EVERY VIOLATION OF CAMP RULES SHOULD BE VISITED WITH THE INFLICTION OF BODILY PAIN IN SOME FORM."

John D. Billings, 10th Massachusetts Artillery

A Cook Confederate carbine and a leather cartridge pouch. Relatively few weapons were actually made by Southern manufacturers, who had neither machinery nor raw materials to produce in quantity. Instead the Confederacy had to rely largely on European imports and captured Federal weapons. *Artifacts courtesy of: Russ Pritchard Collection.*

Many an infraction could bring a transgressor an uncomfortable and humiliating ride on the wooden horse, suffering the ridicule of his camp mates.

Offenders, when punished, were made to ride a wooden horse for hours a day, carry a ball and chain, parade about camp in ridiculous costume, or wear signs proclaiming cowardice, thievery, or desertion. Serious crimes saw a man hanged by his thumbs, or gagged and tied to a wagon wheel, or even branded on the hand or forehead after shaving his hair. Execution was the final punishment, made worse by bungling firing squads that often left it to an officer to fire a *coup de grâce*.

CHAPTER FIVE

The naval conflict

Enlistment for the webfoot Johnny Rebs and Billy Yanks was little different from that of the infantrymen, but after that their training and daily life differed radically. For one thing, more young teenagers, 16 or less, managed to enlist. For another, they were almost always better dressed and supplied, partially because no long marches wore out clothes, while proximity to rivers and harbors made food more readily accessible.

Day to day, the sailor slept in his hammock, rolled it away on rising, then spent the morning swabbing decks, polishing brass, splicing ropes, repairing sails, cleaning the guns, and more. Only then, around 7:30 a.m., did he wash himself and get his breakfast. There followed some leisure hours, perhaps an inspection, then some light gun drill after lunch and before dinner. After that and another inspection, the rest of the day was his for writing letters, listening to a fiddle or banjo player, going ashore if possible, or any of the myriad other amusements by which warriors of all times passed their idle hours.

While it took the Union a while to get up to speed, eventually it was fighting the war on the water with the most modern steam navy in the world.

"THE LIFE OF A SAILOR IS NOT ONE OF A REAL AND REGULAR WORK, . . . YET ITS OUTLINES ARE THE SAME DAY AFTER DAY."

Alvah Hunter, USS Nahant

The navies often saw boys barely into their teens serving as cabin boys and powder "monkeys," like this youth aboard the USS *New Hampshire.*

As with the land forces, the navies had their own distinctive insignia, down to the buttons on their trousers and jackets, like these Yankee buttons from the era.
Artifacts courtesy of: William L. Leigh Collection, Chantilly, Va.

Union seamen aboard the famous USS *Monitor* rest on the deck for midday meal being cooked on the portable stove. Significantly, some of the sailors are black, the navies integrating well before the armies.

A Union seaman proudly poses against a powerful deck gun on a steam frigate. A holdover from earlier naval warfare, cutlasses sit in a rack in the background, though boarding actions were almost nonexistent in this war.

"WITH THE EATING OF THAT FIRST MEAL ABOARD SHIP I BEGAN TO FEEL THAT AT LAST I WAS REALLY SHIPPED INTO THE NAVY."

Alvah Hunter, USS Nahant

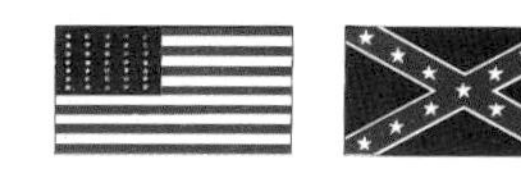

In the officers' mess aboard ship, North or South, a higher class of service was evident, including even monogrammed china. These pieces are from ships of the Confederate Navy.
Artifacts courtesy of: The Museum of the Confederacy, Richmond, Va., and Virginia Historical Society, Richmond, Va.

No one ate like a king in the Civil War, yet in general the men of the navies North and South enjoyed a greater variety and abundance of food at mealtimes than did their counterparts in the armies. Time, content, and quality of meals varied widely according to where a sailor was stationed, but in general he ate three meals a day, starting with breakfast around 7:30a.m., a lunch at noon, and an early dinner around 4 p.m.

The breakfast started with a pint of strong coffee and a large chunk of salt-preserved beef that the sailors derisively called 'junk.' Lunch was the main meal of the day. Much more substantial, it included vegetables, more salt beef or salt pork, anything local like shell fish or game or even fresh meat, cheese, milk, and butter, and the ubiquitous coffee. Sailors on ocean-going commerce raiders sometimes did even better, thanks to what they captured from prizes taken. Finally, thanks to the early hour of serving, dinner was a small meal, perhaps some bread or hardtack, another piece of salt meat, and, of course, coffee.

> "EARLY IN THE MORNING THE JOYFUL CRY OF 'SAIL HO' WAS HEARD FROM THE MASTHEAD."
>
> *George Townley Fullam, CSS* Alabama

The dashing terror of the seas, Captain Raphael Semmes stands at right on the deck of his cruiser the CSS *Alabama*. He sank more Union tonnage than any other Confederate raider.

The USS *Rhode Island*, one of a number of side-wheel steamers used in the Union's ocean-going fleets.

For every hour in actual battle, the average sailor spent weeks or even months in dull routine. The men aboard the river gunboats saw the most action, whether against other vessels or enemy forts. Sailors in the blockading squadrons the Union had stationed off Confederate harbors occasionally chased and took a ship attempting to pass through, but rarely engaged in actual combat, while for Southern sailors in those ports life was much the same. The men on the commerce raiders like the CSS *Alabama* and on the Yankee cruisers hunting them saw most of the oceans of the world, but again little actual fighting.

Instead, for all of them, sea duty meant watching endless miles of river or ocean pass their bows, while remaining ever-vigilant for that speck on the horizon or around the next bend, a hint of sail or a plume of smoke, that could mean the foe approached.

The uniform and equipments of a Confederate naval officer included his tunic, sabers, speaking trumpet, field glasses, compass, pistol, clothes bag, and more. The items here include Captain Semmes' telescope (bottom left) and pistol (bottom right).
Artifacts courtesy of: The Museum of the Confederacy, Richmond, Va., and the Virginia Historical Society, Richmond, Va.

Union sailors aboard one of the *Commodore* class gunboats take a rest during their endless routine of patrolling the rivers and sounds of Virginia and North Carolina.

> "FIRES WERE CROWDED, STEAM INCREASED, . . . BOATS WERE PULLING ABOUT FROM SHIP TO SHIP, SIGNALS WERE FLYING FROM EVERY MAST – FIFTEEN OR TWENTY BOATS LARGE & SMALL RUSHED UP THE RIVER & FORMED IN LINE OF BATTLE BEHIND THE *MONITOR*."
>
> *William F. Keeler, USS* Monitor

No sailor North or South saw as much constant action and danger as the men working the fleets on the Mississippi River and its tributaries, and to a lesser degree the gunboats on Virginia's James River and some of the streams of North Carolina.

Huge behemoth ironclads plied the Mississippi; massive floating 'barns' mounting a dozen guns, powerful steam engines, and carrying a hundred or more men. Even on the hottest summer days they labored in the internal inferno, keeping boilers going even as shipboard temperatures rose above 120 degrees and more. The only respite from the heat was to sleep on deck at night. But on the other hand, they got to go ashore frequently to supplement their food rations with fresh goods, and off either bow the landscape constantly changed, providing some relief from monotony. And working in close conjunction with the armies, they were to witness much of the land war, occasionally even taking their guns ashore as in the siege of Vicksburg to participate in the action.

One of the "infernal machines" that came into its own during the war was the underwater mine, called a "torpedo" at the time, little more than a tin can filled with gunpowder. It was crude but effective. Few ships could withstand a well placed blast under the water line.
Artifacts courtesy of: US Ordnance Museum, Aberdeen Proving Ground, Md.

One of the behemoth Yankee ironclads that patrolled the Mississippi and its lower tributaries in the later stages of the war. These monsters were powerfully armed, heavily armored, and almost impervious to Confederate attack.

Whether his active duty was the monotony of the open sea or the danger of the riverine service, every sailor looked forward to stepping back onto land on a shore pass, and when he did, all too often he came to make sure he was going to have a little fun. No wonder, then, that as with the men in the armies, sailors when given the opportunity found liquor to be a favored release, and that inevitably led to mayhem.

Aboard ship a seaman got a 'grog' ration that only whetted his appetite. 'All insubordination, all misery, every deviltry,' complained a naval official, 'can be traced to *rum*.' Even aboard ship men who hoarded their ration sometimes got drunk; ashore intoxication amongst seamen became epidemic. An 1862 abolishment of the grog ration did not help, but only led to mutiny instead, and its eventual reinstatement. On ship or shore, the boys would be boys.

Articles of clothing and equipment for Union navy officers included frock coats, saber, field glass, sextant, leggings for wet weather, and for a surgeon the white coat, medical kit, and canvas sea bag. *Artifacts courtesy of: The Civil War Library and Museum, Philadelphia, Pa., William Le Pard Collection and Mort Sork Collection.*

One of the Union's workhorse *City* class gunboats that plied the Mississippi. They mounted a dozen guns or more, and bore the brunt of water fighting for the Union for three years on the western waters.

"HE WAS DECIDEDLY ROUGH IN MANNER AND I HAD VISIONS OF TROUBLE, BUT TWO OR THREE OF THE OTHERS HAD COME UP BY THIS TIME AND ONE OF THEM SAID: 'OH! LET HIM ALONE, BILL, HE'S ONLY A KID! IF HE DON'T *WANT* A DRINK DON'T YER MAKE HIM DRINK, AND THERE'S A NIP MORE FOR YOU OR ME, SEE?'"

Alvah Hunter, USS Nahant

Blacks served as enlisted ranks in the Union Navy almost from the outset of the war, and though they could not rise to become officers, still they received a new degree of respect in uniform.

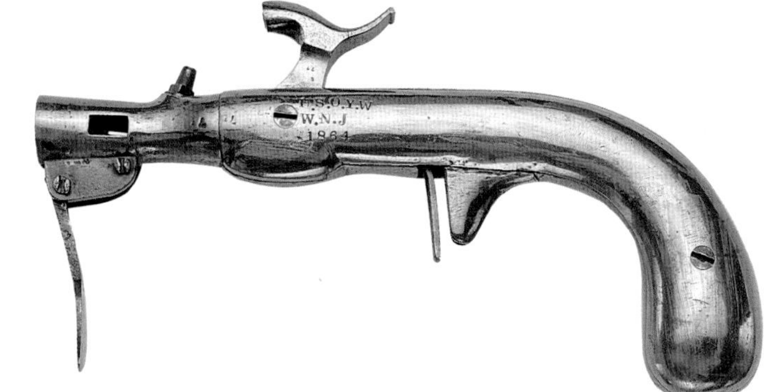

Handguns were a prominent fixture aboard ship, from the officer's LeMat revolver at left, with its separate shotgun barrel beneath the main barrel, to the model 1861 Navy signal pistol at right.
Artifacts courtesy of: Donald Tharpe Collection and Russ A. Pritchard Collection.

> "THERE WERE THREE OR FOUR HUNDRED PEOPLE ON BOARD, AND PROBABLY TWO-THIRDS OF THEM WERE BOYS OF SIXTEEN TO EIGHTEEN YEARS . . . THE WAGES OF A 'FIRST-CLASS BOY' WERE EIGHT DOLLARS PER MONTH."
>
> *Alvah Hunter, USS* Nahant

The crew of a *Commodore* class gunboat, converted from a ferry boat, pose at leisure, listening to the banjo, playing games, whittling sticks. Several of them are black, and more are immigrants.

There was quite a mixture of men aboard the ships, and significantly, sometime before they were allowed to wear the uniform of Union infantrymen, blacks donned the bell-bottomed trousers of Yankee seamen. In September 1861 they began to enlist, and were even given pay equal to white sailors. They served in most of the same capacities in the enlisted grades, acting as cooks, topmen, gun crews, and more, though none rose to officer ranks. In the Confederacy, by contrast, no blacks were officially enlisted, though many served as cooks and servants, and a few even informally helped work the guns when there was need.

Beyond this native born minority, thousands of foreigners served in the navies, especially in the North. Most were north Europeans who came from a seafaring background in Norway, Sweden, or other such countries. Sometimes almost half a ship's complement of crew were foreign born. In the Confederacy, however, most sailors were native born, and with little nautical experience behind them thanks to the absence of a maritime tradition in the South.

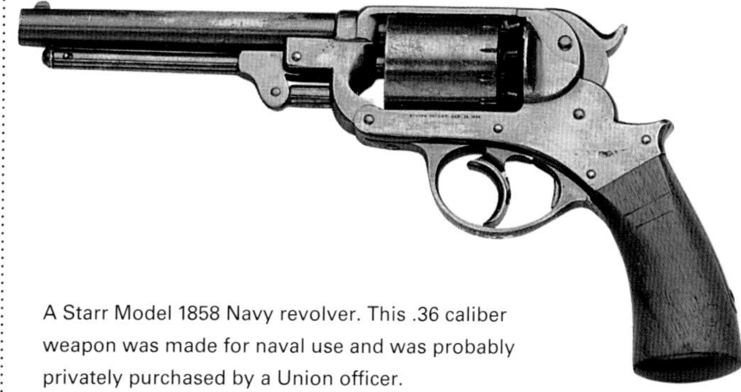

A Starr Model 1858 Navy revolver. This .36 caliber weapon was made for naval use and was probably privately purchased by a Union officer.
Artifact courtesy of: West Point Museum, West Point, NY.

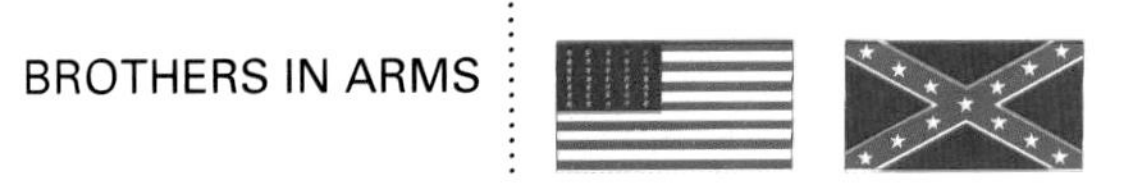

> "WE ARE BEING FURNISHED WITH EVERY POSSIBLE INSTRUMENT OF DESTRUCTION WHICH IT IS SUPPOSED CAN BE OF SERVICE TO US, SHOT, SHELL, SCHRAPNELL, HAND GRENADES, & WROUGHT IRON SHOT . . . WE HAVE GAINED A REPUTATION WE DO NOT AIM TO LOSE."
>
> *William Keeler, USS* Monitor

Sailors in light cotton "duck" trousers pose beside a small deck cannon, beside the "walking beam" of their gunboat's steam engine.

A Dahlgren 12-pounder boat howitzer, one of the standard deck guns in use aboard lighter Union gunboats.
Artifacts courtesy of: Eugene Lomas Collection.

The experience of combat for a sailor differed radically from that encountered by a land soldier. For one thing, many a seaman never actually saw battle, or at best only watched while his ship threw a few shots at a fleeing blockade runner. Most Union ships never came under fire, and most Confederate vessels saw action no more than once or twice before capture or destruction.

But when the seaman did hear the sound of guns, he could feel dreadfully alone, standing on a deck with only a dozen others of his gun crew beside him – not like the infantryman lost in a line of thousands. On the other hand, if he served an ironclad, then he fought his battle within the iron bowels of the ship, blistering hot, grimy from gunsmoke, barely able to see his comrades, and unaware of what was happening outside his gun port, deafened by the din of his gun and the sound of the foe's shot hitting his vessel.

A collection of naval buttons worn on Confederate uniforms, some of imported English brass manufacture, and others of hard rubber for enlisted men.
Artifacts courtesy of: Virginia Historical Society, Richmond, Va.

The gun turret of the mighty ironclad *Monitor*, with some of her officers looking on. She introduced whole new designs into naval architecture, and made history in her duel with the CSS *Virginia*. The dents made by Confederate roundshot can clearly be seen on the turret.

> "ENCOURAGED BY THE GOOD WEATHER, THE MEN GOT OUT THEIR DIDDY-BAGS AND BOXES, BOUGHT BLUE CLOTH OR FLANNEL, SEWING SILK, ETC. OF THE PURSER, AND EMPLOYED THEIR SPARE HOURS IN CUTTING AND MAKING SHIRTS AND TROUSERS."
>
> *Alvah Hunter, USS* Nahant

Items seen aboard every Union warship included the national flag, a variety of cutlasses, an 1842 model Navy pistol, a load of grape shot, and even for a fortunate few, the naval model of the new Medal of Honor.
Artifacts courtesy of: The Civil War Library and Museum, Philadelphia, Pa.

The burden of boredom was probably greater for the sailor than his counterpart in the armies, thanks to his isolation aboard ship or at sea. The sailor's life was an unbroken routine in which one day was no different than the next. Shore leave came with painful infrequency, both because of ships

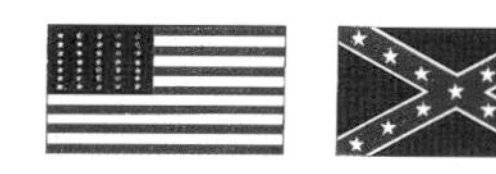

To fight the boredom of shipboard life, sailors turned to music and games, often forming informal ensembles like this one for the entertainment of their shipmates.

A gun crew serves one of the mighty deck guns of a river gunboat, their brooding presence a constant reminder that the naval war was always a serious business.

being at sea for long periods, and also for fear of desertion when in port.

Many turned to drink or found other amusements as they could, or made their own. Gambling proved popular, despite being against regulations, and everyone played the traditional seaman's version of backgammon or 'acey-deucey.' In the evenings the musical instruments came out, the old salts told their exaggerated stories, men boxed or ran foot races on deck, and a few ships even formed theatrical troupes. Now and then on the hot days the captain ordered hoses hooked to the ship's pumps and the men doused themselves playfully to relieve the heat. In the quieter moments, they worked at some small craft, making ropework belts, carving pipes from soapstone, or etching the age-old scrimshaw into a bone. For them, the idle pastimes of the sea had not changed in hundreds of years.

Even generals were captured and imprisoned sometimes. At top is the forage cap of Confederate General Simon Bolivar Buckner, captured at Fort Donelson, Tennessee, and briefly held prisoner. Beneath is the slouch hat of a Confederate lieutenant.
Artifacts courtesy of: The Museum of the Confederacy, Richmond, Va.

CHAPTER SIX

Prisoners of war

At the beginning of the war no one anticipated the demands that prisoners of war would make North and South. The Union at first sent captured Rebels to old masonry fortresses, state prisons, even open air camps, until the demands became so great that special prisons had to be built. By war's end, those camps stretched all across the northern tier of Yankee states, from Elmira, New York, to Rock Island, Illinois, and with places in between like Camp Chase, Johnson's Island, and a score of others.

Men from warm climates like the Confederates were not prepared for the freezing winters in the camps. They received food and blankets and fuel, but often not enough as a parsimonious Washington tried to save money,

A group of captured Confederates pose for the camera at Camp Douglas, outside Chicago, revealing the infinite variety of their attire.

One of the greatest enemies of the prisoner of war was overcrowding. These wooden barracks in a Union prison camp are almost luxurious compared to conditions at some camps, but still disease ran rampant through the compounds.

and later cut back their supplies in retaliation for treatment of Yankee prisoners in the South. No one understood the need for sanitation, of course.

The result was an appalling rate of disease and death. More than 214,000 Confederates fell into Yankee hands and went to prison camps, and at least 25,976 of them never went home again.

"WILL NO ONE SEND A LITTLE WORD TO CHEER US IN OUR GLOOMY HOURS OF ACTIVITY? OH, GOD! HOW DREADFUL ARE THESE BITTER FEELINGS OF HOPE DEFERRED. THUS WE LINGER, THUS WE DRAG THE SLOW, TEDIOUS HOURS OF PRISON LIFE."

Unknown North Carolina Confederate

More of the variety of headgear found among Confederates, in prison and out, from the forage cap of General George W. Randolph above, to a common cap worn by an artilleryman.
Artifacts courtesy of: The Museum of the Confederacy, Richmond, Va.

> **"THE LEXICOGRAPHERS OF OUR LANGUAGE HAVE NOT YET INVENTED THE WORDS OF PROPER STRENGTH TO EXPRESS CONDEMNATION OF THE STUDIED INHUMANITIES OF ANDERSONVILLE."**
>
> *William C. Walker, 18th Connecticut Infantry*

Two fabric covered tin drum water canteens used by Confederates. Men captured took their canteens with them to prison if they could.
Artifacts courtesy of: Virginia Historical Society, Richmond, Va., and the Russ Pritchard Collection.

As bad as things were in the Northern camps, the Yankees captured and sent South suffered even more. Heat, mosquitoes, and the shortages in a Confederacy hard-pressed to feed its own soldiers, conspired to make Southern camps a vision of despair, and of Camp Sumter near Andersonville, Georgia, the incarnation of a millennia of men's speculations on the face of hell.

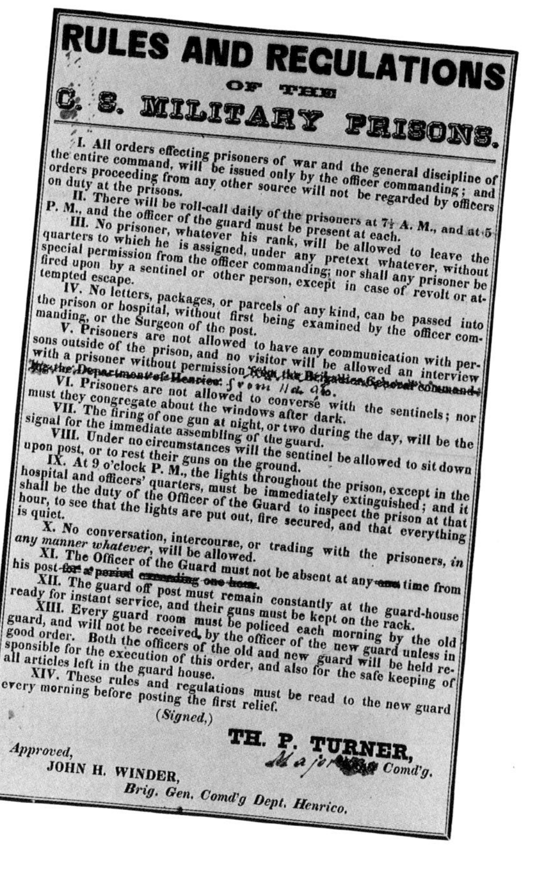

RULES AND REGULATIONS OF THE C. S. MILITARY PRISONS.

I. All orders effecting prisoners of war and the general discipline of the entire command, will be issued only by the officer commanding; and orders proceeding from any other source will not be regarded by officers on duty at the prisons.

II. There will be roll-call daily of the prisoners at 7½ A. M., and at 5 P. M., and the officer of the guard must be present at each.

III. No prisoner, whatever his rank, will be allowed to leave the quarters to which he is assigned, under any pretext whatever, without special permission from the officer commanding; nor shall any prisoner be fired upon by a sentinel or other person, except in case of revolt or attempted escape.

IV. No letters, packages, or parcels of any kind, can be passed into the prison or hospital, without first being examined by the officer commanding, or the Surgeon of the post.

V. Prisoners are not allowed to have any communication with persons outside of the prison, and no visitor will be allowed an interview with a prisoner without permission ~~from the Brigadier General commanding the Department of Henrico~~. from Hd. Qrs.

VI. Prisoners are not allowed to converse with the sentinels; nor must they congregate about the windows after dark.

VII. The firing of one gun at night, or two during the day, will be the signal for the immediate assembling of the guard.

VIII. Under no circumstances will the sentinel be allowed to sit down upon post, or to rest their guns on the ground.

IX. At 9 o'clock P. M., the lights throughout the prison, except in the hospital and officers' quarters, must be immediately extinguished; and it shall be the duty of the Officer of the Guard to inspect the prison at that hour, to see that the lights are put out, fire secured, and that everything is quiet.

X. No conversation, intercourse, or trading with the prisoners, *in any manner whatever*, will be allowed.

XI. The Officer of the Guard must not be absent at any ~~one~~ time from his post ~~for a period exceeding one hour~~.

XII. The guard off post must remain constantly at the guard-house ready for instant service, and their guns must be kept on the rack.

XIII. Every guard room must be policed each morning by the old guard, and will not be received, by the officer of the new guard unless in good order. Both the officers of the old and new guard will be held responsible for the execution of this order, and also for the safe keeping of all articles left in the guard house.

XIV. These rules and regulations must be read to the new guard every morning before posting the first relief.

(*Signed,*)

TH. P. TURNER,
Major Comd'g.

Approved,
JOHN H. WINDER,
Brig. Gen. Comd'g Dept. Henrico.

A broadside proclaiming the rules and regulations to be observed in Confederate military prisons, signed by the commandant of Richmond's infamous Libby Prison, Thomas P. Turner.

The camps only water came from a polluted stream. Its stockade enclosed a mere 26 acres (10 hectares), and surrounded over 30,000 men at its height. The stories of appalling suffering that emerged from that one prison are among the most heart-rending of the war. Many survivors exaggerated, even invented, stories of horror, but the truth was horrific enough. Of the 194,000 Yankees sent to Southern prisons, over 30,000 died, and more than a third of those perished – sometimes at the rate of 139 a day – at Andersonville. The prison actually operated for barely a year, but so impressed itself on the minds of its inmates and the Union that someone had to pay, even if his guilt could be questioned. The noose fell around Major Henry Wirz, Camp Sumter's commander, the only Confederate to be executed for war crimes after the surrenders of 1865.

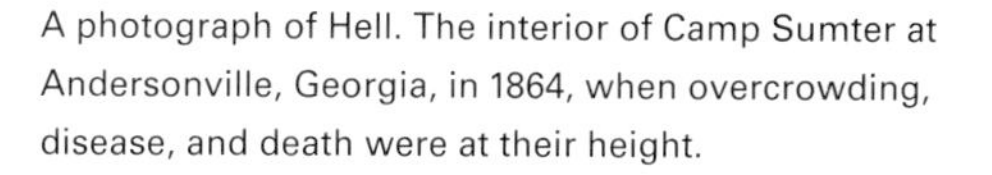

A photograph of Hell. The interior of Camp Sumter at Andersonville, Georgia, in 1864, when overcrowding, disease, and death were at their height.

> "MEN IN THERE WAS JUST AS EVERY PLACE ELSE. SOME HAD NO GET UP ABOUTE THEM, NEVER TRIED TO SHIFT AROUND AND HELP THEMSELVES BUT SIT AROUND DRAW THEIR RASHIONS, GROWL AND TALK ABOUTE HOME AND HOW GOOD MOTHER COULD COOK."
>
> *Captain John W. Lavender, 4th Arkansas Infantry, CSA*

Brigadier General William Hoffman, at right, ran Yankee prisons methodically like an accountant, with the result that his penny-pinching visited unnecessary hardship and suffering on the prisoners in his compounds.

United States Treasury bills circulated to make up for the shortage of hard currency. "Shinplasters," some called them, yet the Confederate prisoner who had a few could buy some much-prized luxuries.
Artifacts courtesy of: CDR James. C. Ruehrmund, USN (Ret). F.R.N.S.

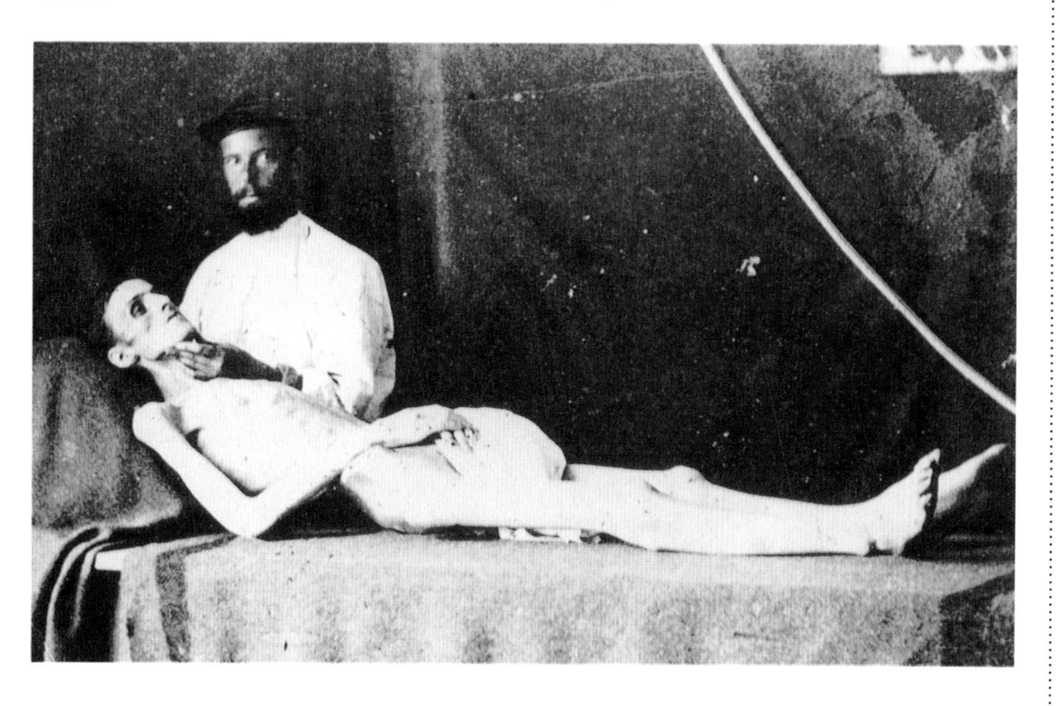

A prisoner released from Andersonville near the end of the war shows the result of malnutrition, inactivity, and disease – chiefly dysentery. Thousands of such living skeletons emerged from prisons both North and South.

On both sides of Mason and Dixon's line, with nothing else to occupy them, prisoners thought and talked constantly about their food. Rations, such as they were, offered the only break in the day's monotony, yet what they ate matched the squalor of their surroundings. Meat came spoiled or fly and worm infested, if it came at all. Maggots and mold often as not covered their bread. One Reb prisoner at Camp Douglas, outside Chicago, believed that his meat ration one day was a piece of mule's neck with the hide and hair still on. Soup like as not came with worms swimming in the weak broth.

No wonder the prisoners went after any scrap of extra nourishment, even if it meant a stray cat or dog, even rats, mice, and birds. An Arkansas soldier ate a 'mess of Fried Rats' and concluded that they resembled squirrels and 'was all right to a hungry man.'

> **"OFTEN WHILE WALKING THE FLOOR OF THE PRISON I REPEAT THE LORD'S PRAYER, AND I FIND MY WHOLE MIND ABSORBED UPON THE SUBJECT OF MY FUTURE STATE OF EXISTENCE OR MY APPEARING BEFORE GOD."**
>
> *William M. Norman, 2d North Carolina Infantry*

A letter from a Confederate prisoner held at Fort Delaware prison. "Pray for me Dayley," it pleads. *Artifact courtesy of: The Museum of the Confederacy, Richmond, Va.*

Fort Delleware U S prison
March the 13th 1865
Dear Wife I Embrace this opertunity
of writing a few lines which if thay Reach you will
inform you that I arived at this place on yesterday
I am very well Except my feet is very sore from
marching we ware captured at Wainsburow Va
on the 2nd inst & we marched to Winchester in 5 Days
[illegible] Evans & W [illegible] were Nearly all of
the Command was captured we have very
good quarters I have not seen James [illegible]
yet I Lost all my clothes blanket I wrote 2 short
letters at Wainsburow to you [illegible]
[illegible] you can cultavate the same
Land in corn & oats we did last year & part
of the meddow Try & Doe the best you can
& Rais all the grain you can Take good care
of those Dear children & keep E K with you
this year if you can get her to stay Keep
your Sperits up & dont trouble yourself
about me I think I can get along very
well & I hope it wont be long till I
can come home write to me when
you get this letter & tel me no how you all are give
my love to all the children & E K pray for me Dayley
from your Husband untill Deth John P. Wilson
To C A Wilson

Old Capitol Prison in Washington was reserved for political prisoners and prominent civilians suspected of disloyalty, often people denied the writ of *habeas corpus*.

Camp Morton, near Indianapolis, Indiana, was one of the largest compounds for Confederate prisoners, and one at which dysentery and a deadly malaise called "the debility" ran rampant.

The hours of confinement crawled past. No prisons provided any sort of organized occupation for their inmates; the men were left entirely to their own devices for recreation. Those who could, wrote, sometimes incessantly. Letters passed the day and helped a man feel a little closer to loved ones and home. Some prisons saw more than 2,000 letters a day being presented to the camp censors for examination and mailing.

The more able-bodied prisoners organized games, foot races, even a variant of baseball, to keep themselves active. A few camps staged theatricals, and others had glee clubs and even a modest camp library. Gambling, of course, passed many an hour, especially between the older prisoners and new ones who still had something to lose. At the other end of the morality scale, religion flourished in the prisons, as men looked to their faith for strength and salvation. But most of all, the men simply sat and talked, and talked, and talked. For many, talk was all they had.

> "We are under the Malishia & ther are the Dambst set of men I ever had the luck to fall in with yet."
>
> *Albert H. Shatzel, 1st Vermont Cavalry*

Inevitably, prisoners regarded their captors as evil incarnate. They told exaggerated stories of the camp at Point Lookout, Maryland, where the commandant Major Allen Brady trampled men under his horse's hooves, or of Fort Delaware's Lieutenant Abraham Wolf exhibiting 'all the mean, cowardly, and cruel instinct of the beast from which his name was taken.'

Buttons worn by state militia in the North. Militia were often used as prison guards, much to the disgust of prisoners, who did not regard them as real soldiers.
Artifacts courtesy of: William L. Leigh Collection, Chantilly, Va.

Guards in the prison yard at Old Capitol Prison. They are assembled for a special occasion, the execution of the conspirators in the Lincoln murder.

An artillery company formed part of the guard garrison at Johnson's Island in Lake Erie, one of the most severe of Union prisons thanks to the weather.

Guards came in for equal execration, and North and South it has to be said that rarely were the best available troops detailed for prison garrison duty. The old or less firm, the inexperienced, and the unreliable in battle, often found themselves stationed as guards. Their captives looked on them as 'the worst looking scallawags,' and soon told exaggerated stories of their cruelties, most of them unfounded.

Yet a few men won the esteem of their prisoners. Colonel Richard Owen commanding Indianapolis' Camp Morton so drove himself to care properly for the Confederates in his camp that they later paid for the placement of a bust of him in the Indiana capitol. And poor Robert Smith commanding Danville, Virginia's prison for Yankees, became so distraught at his inability to care properly for them that he turned to the bottle.

Letters home were the only contact that prisoners of war could maintain with their friends and family, and they were heavily censored before being allowed to pass through the lines.
Artifacts courtesy of: The Museum of the Confederacy, Richmond, Va.

Just a sampling of the myriad handicrafts made by prisoners of war to pass their innumerable idle hours. Anything, a sliver of wood, a chicken bone, a bit of soft stone, could be shaped into something. *Artifacts courtesy of: The Museum of the Confederacy, Richmond, Va.*

For a few of the prisoners nothing could maintain their spirits. At Camp Sorghum, South Carolina, a New York prisoner looked on men who sat 'moping for hours with a look of utter dejection, their elbow upon their knee, and their chin resting upon their hand, their eyes having a vacant, far-away look.' Faced with their condition, short food and bad clothing, the filth and the overcrowding, many simply gave up their grasp on reality and their will to live.

A group of captured Confederates look surprisingly well uniformed as they go into their prison compound. By the time they leave, those left alive will likely be nearly in rags, or else cast-off Union uniforms.

The first prison camps were nothing more than tented encampments like this one at Belle Plain, Virginia, where men were kept until they could be shipped behind the lines to more secure compounds.

Even when these men were finally exchanged or released, the devils in their mind went with them. Tragically, many lived long enough to see freedom, only to die soon after from the effects of their mental torment and their chronic depression. In the end, battle may not have been the ultimate test of character, for imprisonment put untold strains on the mental and physical reserves of the best of men.

> "THE SUFFERINGS OF THE BODY WERE NOT EQUAL TO THE TORTURES OF THE MIND. THE UNCERTAINTY AS TO OUR PROSPECTS OF RELEASE, THE STRANGE SENSE OF ISOLATION FROM THE OUTER WORLD, . . . THE HOPES DEFERRED, . . . THE GRADUAL BUT SURE WEAKENING OF THE BODY – ALL HAD A DEPRESSING EFFECT UPON THE MIND, AND FINALLY MANY BECAME INSANE."
>
> *Leander Cogswell, 11th New Hampshire Infantry*

> “FREEDOM WAS MORE DESIRED THAN SALVATION, MORE SOUGHT AFTER THAN RIGHTEOUSNESS.”
>
> *Abner Small, 16th Maine Infantry*

Simple pastimes like carving wooden spoons, or making a wooden chain, helped keep a prisoner’s mind active and focused, and fought off the deadly lethargy and homesickness that could kill. *Artifacts courtesy of: The Museum of the Confederacy, Richmond, Va.*

For those who held on to their reality and their hope, endless talking helped them through each day, and the most popular – indeed, unceasing – topic was exchange. Early in the war North and South traded prisoners on a one-for-one basis to relieve crowding in prison camps. By 1864, however, the Union halted most exchanges, seeing that it only put men back into the

Shoeless and in rags, Union prisoners of war released from a Confederate compound in Texas testify to the inability of the beleaguered South to care for them well.

Captured officers of the 19th Iowa, as they looked while prisoners at Camp Ford, Tyler, Texas. Nothing remains of their Union outfits. Indeed, they look more "Texan" than their captors.

Confederate armies again where they were much needed, while the Union already had a near-inexhaustible supply of manpower. Still the men in the camps hoped.

'There is considerable excitement this morning about Paroling,' wrote a Minnesota private at Andersonville, 'but it is all gass I reckon for there never was so ignorant a lot of men to gether since the World stood that is in regard to matters outside of the Bull Pen.' Yet for every story dashed, another soon sprang into its place, borne on the winds of rumor and hope. Newly arrived prisoners were pumped for news, any fresh intelligence of peace prospects or of a new exchange cartel. After 1864 very few prisoners were released, and those who were were often so sick they could hardly stand the trip home. It would remain for the end of the war to release them all for good.

"WE FUMED AND FRETTED, AND OUR RESTRAINT GREW MORE AND MORE IRKSOME. AT LAST WE SETTLED DOWN TO THE CONVICTION THAT WE WERE IN FOR THE WAR, UNLESS WE EFFECTED ESCAPE."

Frederick Bartleson, 100th Illinois Infantry

The "shell" jacket of a sergeant in the 6th Pennsylvania Cavalry, the so-called Rush Lancers. Many of the regiment wound up in Rebel prisons. *Artifact courtesy of: West Point Museum, West Point, NY.*

The interior of Libby Prison, the hell hole that kept hundreds of Union officers, and from which scores of them escaped in a daring adventure in 1864.

Escape was on the mind of almost every captive from the moment the enemy took him. Thousands escaped within hours or days of capture, before they could be securely locked behind prison gates. After that moment, however, flight became infinitely more difficult, what with armed guards, tracking dogs, and perhaps hundreds of miles of enemy territory to traverse back to friendly lines.

Still hundreds of men did escape. Mostly they did it by ones and twos, climbing a stockade, or running away while outside the compound on a work party. Some even got away by posing as dead and being transported outside the gates for burial. More spectacular were the attempts at mass breakouts. In December 1864 at the Danville prison camp in Virginia the largest attempt of the war failed when early discovery foiled the plot. More successful was the breakout by Union officers from Richmond's Libby Prison. On February 9, 1864, more than 100 Yankees crawled out through a tunnel, and 58 made good their flight to friendly lines.

Libby Prison, photographed in 1863, with Union prisoners peering out from its upper windows, and part of the Confederate guard drawn up in line below.

CHAPTER SEVEN

Bloody work ahead

None of them knew what to expect on the eve of battle, especially if it was their first. The night before the first Battle of Bull Run, in 1861, a Yankee mused that it was particularly beautiful. 'The sky is perfectly clear, the moon is full and bright, and the air is as still as if it were not within a few hours to be disturbed by the roar of cannon and the shouts of contending men.' Bands sometimes played. Men wrote letters home, filled in their diaries, even pinned their names and addresses inside their uniforms in case they should fall.

Mostly they sat at their campfires, relieving the tension by singing, telling old stories, reliving battles past. Some turned fatalistic. 'Often at the still hour of midnight,' said one Rebel, 'I wish the next day will be the "cross-over", and we will meet the "grand army" on fair ground.'

Small flags seen on every battlefield of the war, these pennants designated headquarters of units from brigade to corps. The pennant on the right is the designation flag of the Union brigade which held Cemetery Ridge during the last day of the Battle of Gettysburg.
Artifacts courtesy of: The Union League of Philadelphia.

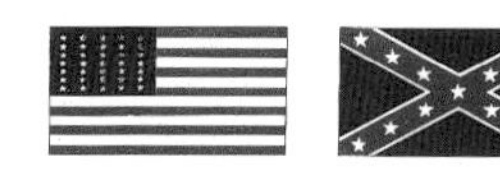

In Virginia in 1862 a Union regiment parades before its encampment. It was in much the same ranks that these men would go into battle.

"I HAVE A MORTAL DREAD OF THE BATTLE FIELD FOR I HAVE YET BEEN NEARER TO ONE THAN TO HEAR THE CANNON ROAR & HAVE NEVER SEEN A PERSON DIE."

Private Edward Edes, Massachusetts Infantry, USA

"IF YOU SEE ANYONE THAT SAYS THEY WANT ANY AFRAID YOU MAY KNOW THAT IT WANT ME."

A Maine Infantryman, USA

An early 1861 image showing Confederates in Fort McRee, outside Pensacola, Florida; men who have yet to hear the first sound of a gun fired in anger.

Typical belt plates worn by Confederates; both were used predominantly among the armies in the East.

Going into battle for the infantryman, whether his first time or his fiftieth, seemed much the same. There was the pre-dawn reveille, though most likely he was already awake, mouth dry, hands sweaty and shaking slightly with nervous anticipation. Once the firing started, however, time oddly seemed to fly and most of the nervousness disappeared. 'Time rolls off very fast in time of battle,' said one Confederate.

When the moment came for the men to go into battle, they formed line at the command, made certain their weapons were loaded and bayonets fixed, and moved forward. The excitement was almost too much for some, and men suffering from diarrhea – which could be half a regiment at a time – feared they might embarrass themselves in action. Most did not.

Answering orders transmitted by voice, bugle, or drum, they moved into the battleline. They could not fire yet, though the enemy might be firing at them. The tension mounted intolerably. 'Oh dear!' a Yankee cried, 'when shall *we* fire?' When at last they did, it was an enormous relief.

The equipment of the Confederate infantryman as he went into battle. He carried his rifle, sometimes a Bowie knife, a canteen, cartridge and cap boxes, haversack with rations, and wore the uniform and boots if he had them.
Artifacts courtesy of: Virginia Historical Society, Richmond, Va.

In these siege works around Atlanta, Union artillery was well placed to batter the city's defenders.

A stand of grape shot was nothing more than nine large iron balls that flew apart when fired from a cannon, bringing down men and animals. The 7-inch shell above was filled with powder, and activated by a fuze in the top that could be set for distances. *Artifacts courtesy of: West Point Museum, West Point, NY.*

"WE ARE REQUIRED TO MOVE THE GUNS ABOUT BY HAND, OVER THE FIELD, TO FRONT AND TO REAR, IN ECHELON AND IN LINE, TO SPONGE AND LOAD AND FIRE IN MIMIC WARFARE, UNTIL OUR ARMS ACHE, AND WE LONG FOR REST."

Benjamin W. Jones, Surry [Virginia] Light Artillery, CSA

The artillery was the overlooked branch of the service, neither so numerous or important as the infantry, nor as colorful as the cavalry. Yet some 700 batteries and battalions formed North and South, and on virtually every battlefield of the war was heard the report of their cannon, from little 6-pounder howitzers, to mammoth siege guns and mortars firing shot and shell weighing hundreds of pounds.

The gunner rarely stood on the front line, unless the enemy drove back his infantry supports and charged his battery. For most of them, battle meant firing solid shot at the foe's cannon hundreds of yards away, then exploding shells to disrupt his infantry line and soften it for his own infantry to assault, or else grape and canister loads – like huge shotgun shells – into an attacking line of the foe. His greatest danger was from enemy cannon, or from being run over by an infantry charge. His greatest fear was the loss of his guns, symbol of his pride in his battery.

A Union artilleryman went into battle often covered with color, from the red facings on his blue shell jackets, to the brass eagle on his Hardee hat. Some carried Roman shot swords, and had pistols with which to defend their guns when attacked.

"It was, indeed, a magnificent sight as the long column of many thousand horsemen stretched across this beautiful Potomac . . . There were few moments, perhaps, from the beginning to the close of the war, of excitement more intense, of exhilaration more delightful."

Heros Von Borke, Staff of General, J.E.B. Stuart, CSA

This Yankee cavalryman may not look too dashing, but he represents tens of thousands of intrepid men, North and South, who went to war on horseback.

A guidon of the 6th Pennsylvania Cavalry, Rush Lancers, displaying some of their battle credits. *Artifacts courtesy of: The Civil War Library and Museum, Philadelphia, Pa.*

All the romance of the war, it seemed, rested in the imagery surrounding the bold cavalryman. Young men dreamed of the gaudy uniform, the curved saber at his side, the jaunty oversize boots, and the adulation the ladies instinctively felt for the bold 'cavalier', so dashing in the charge.

The reality of the cavalryman's experience of combat was considerably different. Rarely did the horsemen actually fight on horseback. A mounted man could hardly hit a thing with his carbine or pistol when in motion, and most quickly discarded their sabers as absolutely useless for anything but roasting joints of meat over campfires.

When he did fight, the trooper rode to the battlefield, then dismounted, one man holding the horses of four, while the other three fought on foot. Only rarely, as at Brandy Station, Virginia, in 1863, did cavalry meet cavalry on horseback and engage in charge and countercharge.

The Union cavalryman went into the fight clad in his shell jacket with yellow trim, carrying a Spencer carbine if fortunate, a model 1860 saber, and mounted on a McClellan saddle. The lance, though carried by the 6th Pennsylvania at the beginning of the conflict, was a European weapon that would find no lasting place in this American war.
Artifacts courtesy of: J. Craig Nannos Collection and The Civil War Library and Museum, Philadelphia, Pa.

"AFTER THE FIRST ROUND THE FEAR LEFT ME & I WAS AS COOL AS EVER I WAS IN MY LIFE. I THINK I HAVE BEEN A GREAT DEAL MORE EXCITED IN ATTEMPTING TO SPEAK A PIECE IN SCHOOL OR TO MAKE REMARKS IN AN EVENING MEETING."

Herbert E. Valentine, Massachusetts Infantryman, USA

Contrary to all expectation at the time, and romanticizing later, very little hand-to-hand fighting took place in the war. Rather, one side or the other launched assaults with part of its line, and either they were beaten back by musket and artillery fire before they reached an enemy line, or else the foe lost heart or saw itself about to be overpowered, and withdrew before actual physical contact occurred.

They moved at double-time – 165 steps a minute – though some men tried to go even faster, and when they moved they seemed to lean forward, as if facing a terrible wind, as indeed they were. Their bayonets might frighten a foe, but they rarely used them. Instead, they fired their rifles, sometimes wildly in the confusion. 'I acted like a madman,' one Pennsylvanian remembered. 'A kind of desperation seized me . . . I jumped over dead men with as little feeling as I would over a log. The feeling that was uppermost in my mind was a desire to kill.'

That was battle.

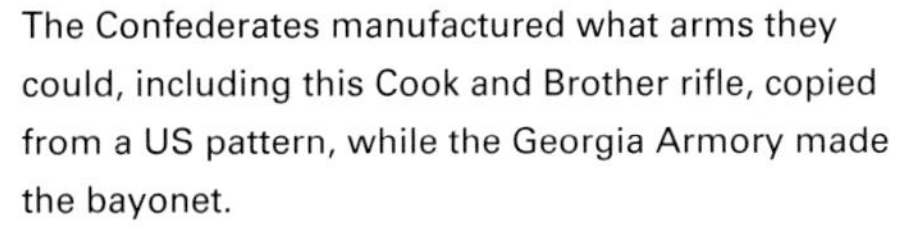

The Confederates manufactured what arms they could, including this Cook and Brother rifle, copied from a US pattern, while the Georgia Armory made the bayonet.
Artifacts courtesy of: Russ Pritchard Collection

Some of the cost of war. These Union soldiers fell in battle at Gettysburg, and passing Confederates have removed their boots.

Packets of musket and rifle cartridges were given to the soldiers sometimes. At left are huge .69 caliber round ball loads, while the other two are Merrill carbine cartridges; all three boxes were made in the Confederacy.
Artifacts courtesy of: Virginia Historical Society, Richmond, Va., and The Museum of the Confederacy, Richmond, Va.

> "To mass troops against the fire of a covered line is simply to devote them to destruction. The greater the mass, the greater the loss – that is all."
>
> *Gen. John M. Schofield, USA*

The scene of carnage behind the stone wall on Marye's Heights in May 1863. During the fighting around Chancellorsville, Virginia, the Heights became the focus for bitter fighting, the results of which were eloquently captured later by a Yankee photographer.

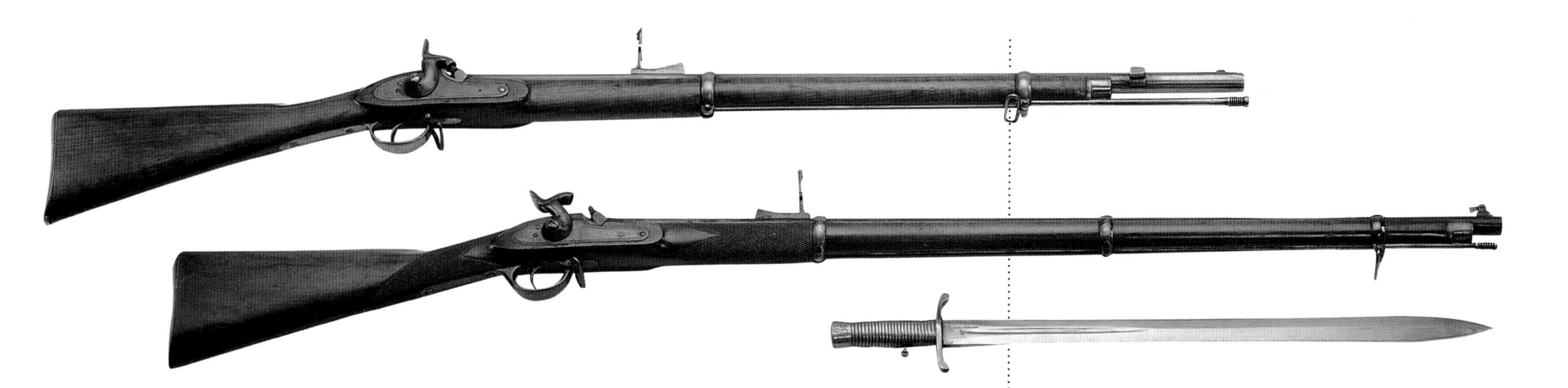

Imported rifles like these British guns became important to a Confederacy unable to make enough of its own. At top is an 1853 short rifle, and beneath is a Kerr's patent rifle. The sword bayonet is also an import.
Artifacts courtesy of: Virginia Historical Society, Richmond, Va.

Warfare had changed between America's last war – the one with Mexico in 1846–48 – and the Civil War. For centuries, commanders depended on the attack to win battles, something they could do thanks in part to the ineffectiveness of their firearms. But by 1861 the introduction of rifled shoulder arms, used almost universally North and South, changed that. They fired farther, faster, and with greater accuracy.

Now the attacker, moving over open ground, was a prime target for perhaps several hundred yards, while the defender, behind the security of a fence, a barricade, or even an earthwork, could send volley after volley at him, and with telling effect even allowing for the poor marksmanship of Reb and Yank. The infantry assault was not quite made obsolete, but for every one that succeeded in this war, half a dozen or more failed. Men, for all their bravery and determination, simply could not stand the volume of fire they faced. Truly it was a wind, a deadly breeze of lead.

Several of the cartridges needed to keep the armies killing. They range from the standard .58 load at far left, to a .69 ball next to it, a .50 Smith, a .52 Sharps, a .54 Burnside, a .50 Maynard, a .52 Sharps and Hankins, and at right a .44 Henry rifle bullet. The variety of ammunition used by both sides in the war was enormous.
Artifacts courtesy of: The Civil War Library and Museum, Philadelphia, Pa.

> "FOR SOME TIME THE CHEERS AND ACTIONS OF THE MEN ARE STRONGLY CONTRASTED WITH THEIR APPEARANCE A FEW SHORT HOURS BEFORE. MEN WHO COULD HARDLY KEEP IN THE LINE NOW SHOUT AND RUN AROUND ALMOST CRAZY WITH JOY."
>
> *Alexander G. Rose, New York Infantryman*

The national colors of the 3d Pennsylvania Cavalry display proudly all of the battles and skirmishes in which it participated.
Artifact courtesy of: The Civil War Library and Museum Philadelphia, Pa.

More often than not, the soldiers on the winning side did not realize at first that theirs was the victory. They could only see one portion of a battleline that could stretch for miles, often through tangled and wooded country. Indeed, a man seeing the enemy standing firm in his front, knew nothing for a time of the triumphs that might have happened on either side of him. Only gradually, in most cases, did victors realize their fortunes, usually at first by seeing the enemy in their front retire hastily, and then by the sounds of cheering in their own distant lines, a swelling shout that soon swept over the entire army. Soon after this first realization might come an order to charge, to pursue the fleeing foe. Forward they would go at a run, and thankfully it all now happened too fast for any to think about what he was doing. Instead of reloading, some men picked up fallen rifles on the way and hurled themselves at remaining enemy. The shouting, the stabbing, the clubbing and firing, were soon over.

At the end of the war, when the veterans returned home, they brought their proud and tattered old colors with them; some like these were reduced to little more than shreds.

Standing and sitting atop Lookout Mountain, overlooking Chattanooga and the Tennessee River, Union veterans of the armies of the west display the guns that have served them in many a battle, and the colors they followed into the fight.

> "IF I HADENT SEEN THE FIX I WAS IN, AND RUN LIKE BLAZES, I WOULD HAVE BEEN A GONER BY THIS TIME."
>
> *William H. Lloyd, New Jersey Infantryman, USA*

Nothing could be more demoralizing, after all the preparation, facing and overcoming the fear and anxiety, than to be a part of a defeated army. He had seen friends shot and killed, perhaps even brothers or sons, and all for nothing. He may have lost his weapon, or seen his army's proud artillery captured or destroyed. In time there came a relief at being still alive, but the first emotions were of anger and shame.

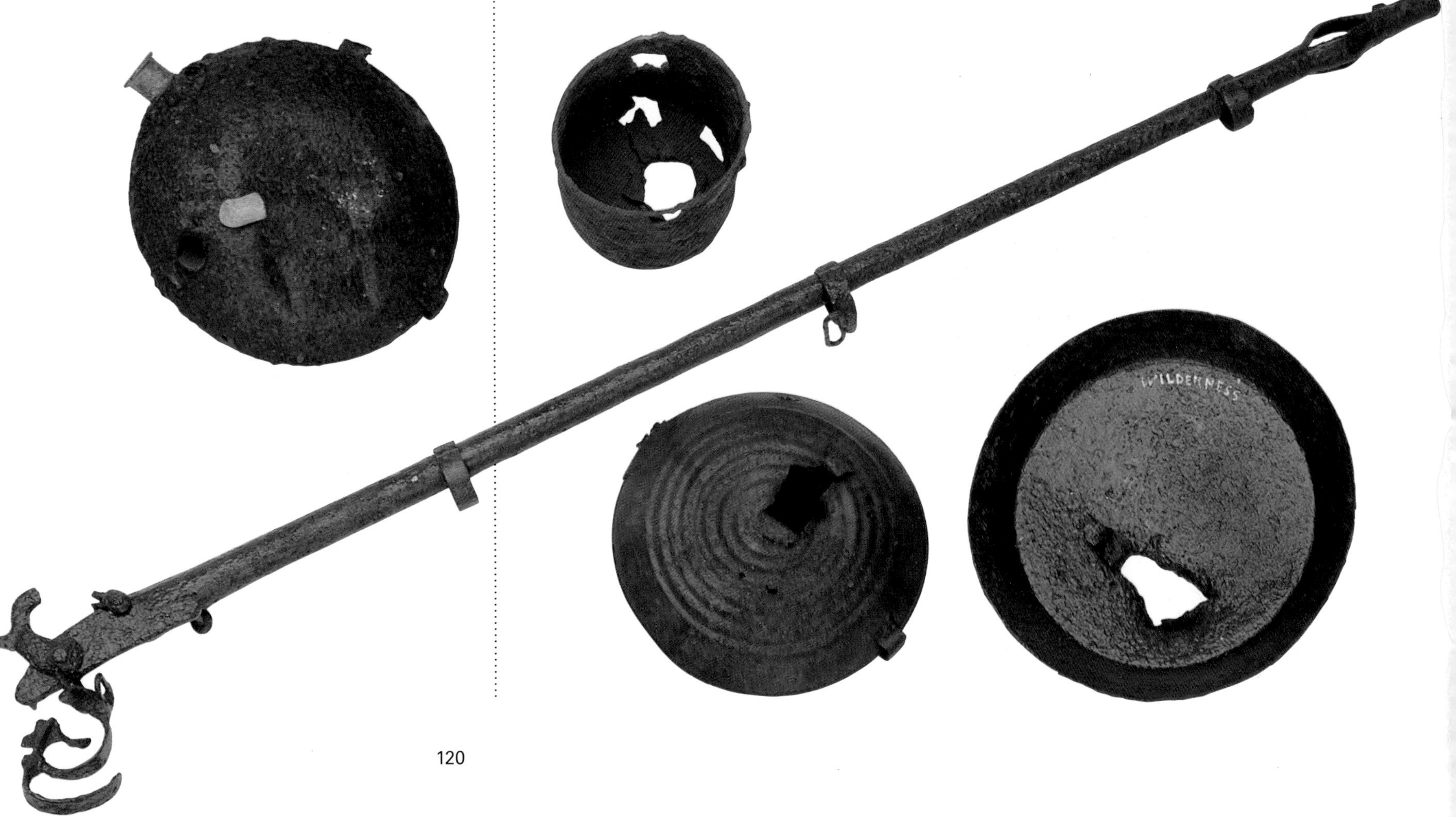

Artifacts found on the battlefields years after the war leave a haunting reminder that the armies passed this way, from the tin cup and broken plate, to the canteen with a bullet hole, and the model 1861 Springfield rifle with its burst barrel.
Artifacts courtesy of: Wendell Lang Collection, Tarrytown, NY.

Worse reminders lay in the ground, like these skeletons of Union dead found near Cold Harbor during the war, and now being properly reinterred.

Even those feelings, however, had to wait until the confusion and disorientation abated. Put to flight, a reatreating army often bore little resemblance to the disciplined machine that had approached the field. Now men fled in panic, organization disintegrated, officers were ignored, and some men even threw down their weapons in the haste to get to safety. As the war progressed and men gained more experience, most learned to swallow defeat with equanimity, but still, even as late as November 1863 at Missionary Ridge, Tennessee, a Confederate army could be sent in utter panic from the field.

> "ALL ALONG THE ROUTE BY WHICH THIS TRAIN MADE ITS WAY, BROKEN WAGONS AND DEAD AND DYING SOLDIERS WERE STREWED. THE BOTTOM OF THE WAGONS WAS SMEARED WITH BLOOD . . . THE VASTNESS OF THE TRAIN, AND THE AGGREGATE OF HUMAN AGONY IT CONTAINED, HAS NEVER BEEN UNDERSTOOD."
>
> *Jacob Hoke, Pennsylvania resident*

These field artillery shells are of Confederate manufacture. The brass cups and plates at the base of the shells were crude methods of engaging the rifling in the gun's barrel on firing.
Artifacts courtesy of: West Point Museum, West Point, NY.

Lines of dead await a hasty burial after the battle of Antietam. One of the bloodiest days of the war left over 22,000 casualties scattered over the fields around the small Maryland village of Sharpsburg.

Excavated Confederate side knives and a Bowie knife. Though useless in the face of musket bullets and cannon shells, side knives were still popular. *Artifacts courtesy of: The Wendell Lang Collection, Tarrytown, N.Y.*

There must have been many civilians who thought that the war would never come near them, . Abraham Trostle built his home at Gettysburg, only to have it swept by the Confederate advance on the second day of the battle. In a few hours his farm was transformed into a carrion field.

Once the armies had gone, every battlefield was a butcher's yard. Thousands of dead animals littered the land, amongst the wreckage of cannon and wagons, broken weapons, and bits and pieces of men. It took months to clean up after Gettysburg, and even then for a long time the stench of sulfur and rotting flesh, animal and human, forced visitors to breathe through their handkerchiefs. Vast humanitarian efforts had to be mounted to get the dead men and animals buried, often where they fell just to prevent disease. The work of identifying those who could be recognized would take longer, and for months – years – afterward there would come the sad-eyed relatives in their wagons, hoping to find a son or brother to take him home. As for the communities themselves, sometimes they never completely erased the scars of battle, whether on the landscape or in the memories of their people.

CHAPTER EIGHT

Countrymen again

When at last the war was over, the Union victory won, the men in blue experienced the fullest possible gamut of emotion. Certainly there was the heady feeling of having been the winner. Men cheered, some fired their guns in celebration, yet most met the news with quiet, and a surprising quotient of compassion for the men they had beaten. All felt a profound sense of relief. 'Never shall I forget the feeling that passed over my soul just before retiring,' wrote one Ohioian the day in April Robert E. Lee's

When it was all over, the Union celebrated with a Grand Review of its armies in Washington. They paraded past this grand stand, before the eyes of President Andrew Johnson and his cabinet.

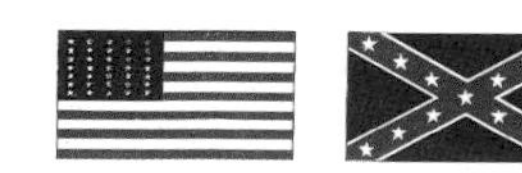

> **"I REMEMBER HOW WE SAT THERE AND PITIED AND SYMPATHIZED WITH THESE COURAGEOUS SOUTHERN MEN WHO HAD FOUGHT FOR FOUR LONG AND DREARY YEARS ALL SO STUBBORNLY, SO BRAVELY AND SO WELL, AND NOW, WHIPPED, BEATEN, COMPLETELY USED UP, WERE FULLY AT OUR MERCY."**
>
> *S. Thompson, 13th New Hampshire Infantry, USA, 1865*

The victorious leaders received every manifestation of their people's gratitude. General George G. Meade, commander of the Army of the Potomac, was given this gold commemorative medal.
Artifacts courtesy of: The Civil War Library and Museum, Philadelphia, Pa.

Confederate army surrendered; 'the knowledge that *now* we could go to bed & *feel sure* of enjoying a full night's rest.'

Yankees surprised themselves at the absence of vindictive feeling toward their vanquished enemy, and at how quickly all hostility evaporated after the war officially finished. They had never wanted to fight. Now that it was done, they could not wait to put it all behind them.

Major General Francis Preston Blair received a deluxe presentation sword and scabbard, the customary sign of reward from constituents and public spirited citizens.
Artifact courtesy of: The Civil War Library and Museum, Philadelphia, Pa.

> "BLOW, GABRIEL, BLOW! MY GOD, LET HIM BLOW, I AM READY TO DIE!"
>
> *A North Carolina Infantryman, CSA*

Defeat was something that Confederates could see all around them in 1865. Much of Richmond lay in ruins after disastrous fires and the destruction of military warehouses.

Left: The ravages of the war showed in the Confederates' flags, like this banner of the First Kentucky "Orphan" Brigade. Carried all across the South, it, like its men, lay in tatters.
Artifact courtesy of: The Museum of the Confederacy, Richmond, Va.

More than any other man except perhaps Abraham Lincoln, it was General U.S. Grant who finally brought the Confederacy to its knees, and the war to an end. This photograph was taken less than a month before General Lee's surrender.

No Americans had ever been defeated in a war, but now the South had. Worse, they had had a proud military tradition. Now they were beaten. 'I wish I could go out in the woods and die drunk and bury all my sorrows,' a Kentuckian lamented, while another Reb exclaimed that 'this was the blackest day of our lives.'

After the first shock, however, most felt a sudden sense of collapse, physical and mental, that lasted for hours. They spoke very little, but merely sat or lay on the ground, contemplative, trying to sort their emotions at the irrefutable end of their four-year struggle. If they did talk, it was to comfort and reassure each other that every man had done his best, they had fought a good fight, and that there was no shame in defeat. Some could not do that, though, and melted into the countryside. A very few actually took their own lives. But for most their only last act of resistance was to bash their rifles against tree trunks and bury their banners rather than see them surrendered.

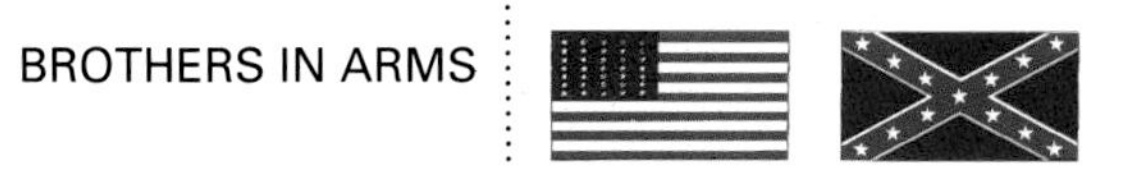

One of the rocks upon which the South foundered was economics. The Confederacy bravely tried to finance itself with bonds, loans tied to planters' cotton, even treasury notes, but in the end it was not nearly enough.
Artifacts courtesy of: The Civil War Library and Museum, Philadelphia, Pa.

> **"WE WILL GO HOME, MAKE THREE MORE CROPS, AND TRY THEM AGAIN."**
>
> *An anonymous Confederate*

The last national flag of the Confederacy. This third design was adopted in March 1865 barely a month before the South's surrender. It was little more than a gesture of defiance.
Artifact courtesy of: The Museum of Confederacy, Richmond, Va.

Some simply could not accept defeat. When Robert E. Lee surrendered the Army of Northern Virginia, some men slipped away and went into North Carolina to join the Army of Tennessee, and when it surrendered two weeks later, some groups refused to be included in the terms. Instead, they moved on, hoping somehow to link with other small bands, or to make it to the remaining Confederate army west of the Mississippi. Confederate President Jefferson Davis himself encouraged this, and in his own escape attempt vowed that they could continue the fight as partisans and prolong the contest for years until the Yankees gave up chasing them.

It was a futile and unrealistic hope. Partisans could only operate in a region where there was a friendly civilian population to suppport them. With all of the coastal areas under Yankee control, Confederates would have had to retreat to the hill and mountain country in the interior, regions where Unionism always ran strong. Cut off from seaports and foreign aid, and unable to make their own weapons and supplies, Confederate guerillas would have found the Yankees in their front and unsympathetic Southerners in their rear.

With the Confederacy collapsing, President Davis hoped to continue the war on horseback with partisans and raiders like the indomitable General Nathan Bedford Forrest. It was a futile and pointless hope.

> "WELL, SIR, WHERE ARE YOU GOING?"
> HOME, SIR, HOME.
>
> *General Robert McAllister and a Union Private*

At the time of the Confederate collapse, the Union Army had 1,034,000 men enlisted and under arms. How were all these men who had been soldiers for so long to be returned to civilian life? No one had any experience with disbanding a force of this size. Units from some states were more than a thousand miles from home, and any state's regiments could be scattered throughout the several field armies. Consequently each corps had to be broken down regiment by regiment and its men sent home in small groups. Then the War Department had to see to the final pay due the soldiers and provide for transportation home.

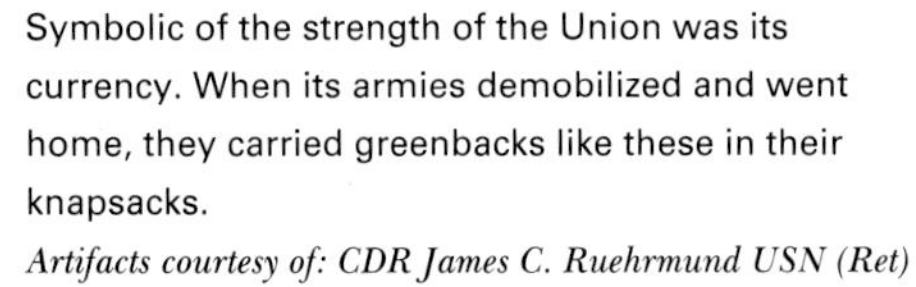

Symbolic of the strength of the Union was its currency. When its armies demobilized and went home, they carried greenbacks like these in their knapsacks.

Artifacts courtesy of: CDR James C. Ruehrmund USN (Ret) F.R.N.S.

Pennsylvania Avenue in Washington was the last march for many of the Yankees, as they passed down the street in the grand Review in May. Behind them lay not only the war, but the great adventure of their lives.

It was a Herculean task, yet one accomplished with amazing efficiency and in record time. More than $270,000,000 was disbursed on the final pay days and more than three-quarters of a million men transported and discharged within six months of the last surrenders. By February 1866 the United States Army was down to 80,000. For the rest, the last day of service was a bitter-sweet reunion with old comrades, the leaving of one way of life to take up another.

Thanks to the scarcity of hard currency in gold and silver, the Union even issued fractional notes like these for 10, 25, and 50 cents.
Artifacts courtesy of: CRD James C. Ruehrmund USN (Ret) F.R.N.S.

"I AM DAILY TOUCHED TO THE HEART BY SEEING THESE POOR HOMESICK BOYS AND EXHAUSTED MEN WANDERING ABOUT IN THREADBARE UNIFORMS, . . . SEEKING THE NEAREST ROUTE HOME; THEY HAVE A CARE-WORN AND ANXIOUS LOOK, A PLAYED-OUT MANNER."

New York Tribune *correspondent*

Few Confederates managed to survive the war with their uniforms as pristine as this Louisiana soldier's frock coat or the shell jacket. Nevertheless the remains of the uniform in which they marched home were symbols of their cause, and proudly worn. *Artifacts courtesy of: Don Troiani Collection.*

Generous in victory, many Union commanders opened well stocked commissary wagons like these to the hungry Confederates before they made their long march home.

How different it was for the Confederate soldiers after the surrenders. No pay, no transportation, no cheering crowds for them. After turning over his weapon and giving his parole, he was on his own. Generous victors like Grant and Sherman did open their commissaries to the Southerners, and let those who claimed to own animals take them from Rebel wagons and cannon. But how a Confederate soldier made his way back home was exclusively his own business. The Union gave ship transportation as far as New Orleans or Galveston to some who lived west of the Mississippi, while some others occasionally found compassion in a military railroad or wagon train commander.

But mostly they walked, sometimes hundreds of miles. The roads of the South almost choked with the soldiers trudging homeward, passing through a land strained to the breaking point by the war. When they asked at farmhouses for food and water, there was little to give. Worse, all along the war they could see the destruction the war wrought on their homeland. Truly theirs was a trail of tears.

For many a Johnny Reb, the only souvenirs he would have would be the buttons he saved from the ruins of his uniform.
Artifacts courtesy of: Virginia Historical Society, Richmond, Va.

> "THERE IS COMPLETE REVULSION IN PUBLIC FEELING. NO MORE TALK ABOUT HELP FROM FRANCE AND ENGLAND, BUT ALL ABOUT EMIGRATION TO MEXICO AND BRAZIL. WE ARE IRRETRIEVABLY RUINED."
>
> *Eliza F. Andrews, Georgia*

Scenes like these ruins in South Carolina were simply too much for some of the defeated to bear. Rather than see them, or try to rebuild in the new America, they chose exile instead.

Some embittered Southerners burned their flags, or buried them, or tore them into pieces as souvenirs, rather than surrender them. Happily, these banners survived as symbols of the sacrifices of their followers.
Artifacts courtesy of: The Museum of the Confederacy, Richmond, Va.

Some of course, simply could not give up, or the trip home was simply too much to face. Too proud to concede defeat, and too bitter to live under Yankee rule, they headed toward the Rio Grande where 5,000 or more joined with a few generals to cross the border and offer their services to Mexico. Eventually many of them started colonies at Carlotta and elsewhere.

Others went even farther from home, to Central America, Venezuela, Brazil, and other Latin countries, while still more crossed the ocean to Europe, taking residence in England and France. Some took service in the army of the Khedive of Egypt. More journeyed to the Far East, and several hundred recrossed the Atlantic to settle in Canada, within sight of the United States. It was the largest expatriation movement in American history, but it did not last. Eventually all but a few of the 10,000 or more exiles returned to the South, realizing that their best future lay not in rejecting America, but in rebuilding it.

Most men North and South seemed to understand instinctively that the best hope for all of them lay in reconciliation, in putting the past behind them as quickly as possible. While President Davis vainly tried to carry on before he was captured, and while others disappeared into the Southern hills or left for foreign shores, most Confederate leaders counseled otherwise. Men like General Robert E. Lee told their one-time soldiers to accept the verdict of the war, go home, and start building the South anew.

From the first, these former Rebel leaders tried to instill in the men a sense of pride in what they had done, what they stood, fought, and died for. Failure only ennobled their sacrifice and their cause. Defeat did not mean dishonor, and in no time the old soldier wit returned as Confederate veterans quipped that they were never really *defeated*, they just 'wore ourselves out whipping the Yanks.'

A type of National Bunting flag displayed by ships of the Union Navy during the war.
Artifact courtesy of: The Civil War Library and Museum, Philadelphia, Pa.

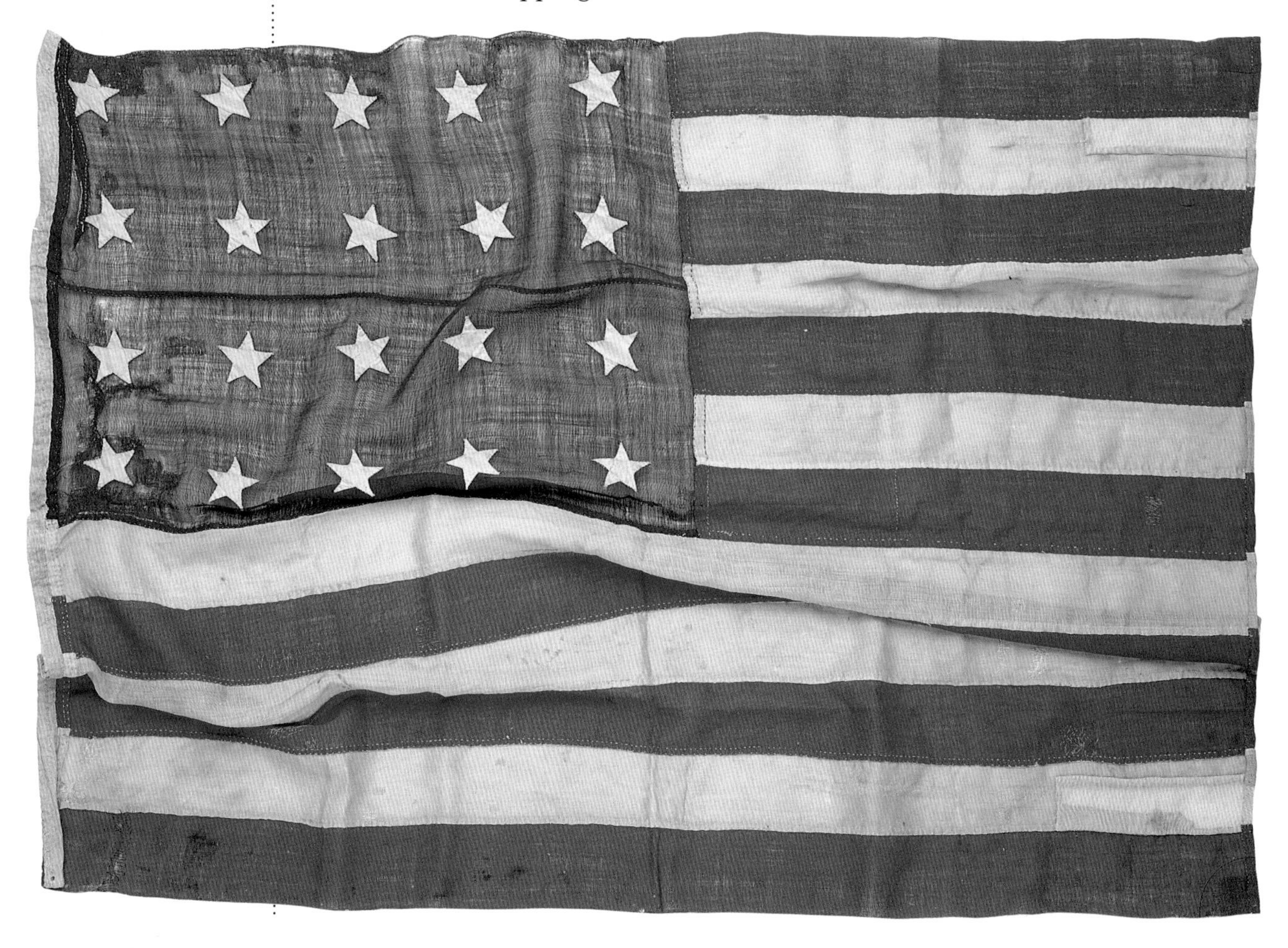

Years after the war, old Confederates live and remember in a soldiers' home in Kentucky, reliving their battles and the days of their youth.

Andrew Johnson succeeded Lincoln to the Presidency after the assassination, and attempted to effect peaceful reconciliation in spite of embittered feelings North and South.

"WAR IS HELL BROKE LOOSE AND BENUMBS ALL THE TENDER FEELINGS OF MEN AND MAKES OF THEM BRUTES. I DO NOT WANT TO SEE ANY MORE SUCH SCENES AND YET I WOULD NOT HAVE MISSED THIS FOR ANY CONSIDERATION."

Sergeant Cyrus P. Boyd, 15th Iowa Infantry, USA

The Army version of the Medal of Honor.
Artifact courtesy of: The Civil War Library and Museum, Philadelphia, Pa.

The soldiers themselves created the best memorials to their deeds, as in the decades after the war they began erecting monuments all across the battlefields North and South, places to remember and honor what they had done. This particular memorial was erected at Gettysburg 20 years after the battle.

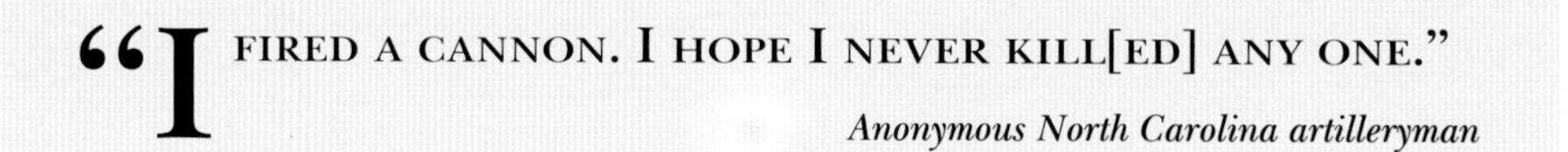

"I FIRED A CANNON. I HOPE I NEVER KILL[ED] ANY ONE."

Anonymous North Carolina artilleryman

They paid a terrible price. More than 623,000 men lost their lives, most of them to disease. At least another 471,000 wounded. In more than 10,000 actions, from tiny forgotten skirmishes to the mighty battles like Gettysburg, they drew each other's blood. In the Union, by the end, the war was costing almost $4 million a day, to a total cost of $1,295,100,000 for 1865 alone. All

told the Union probably spent over $4 billion. The South spent nearly $4 billion, most of which it borrowed and could never repay. Beyond this, none could calculate the cost of the damage done to Southern industry, railroads, cities, and agriculture. Most of South's resources had been layed waste, and it would take generations to rebuild.

Yet rebuild they would, and despite the strains of Reconstruction, and then the decades of agitation over civil rights and the place of the now free blacks in Southern and American society, they would do it for the most part together. As John C. Breckinridge, once United States Vice President, then Confederate general and secretary of war, said in 1866 just after the surrenders, 'It is all right and far better that we live as one people.' Now, again, one people they would be.

The Naval version of the Medal of Honor, in its case.
Artifact courtesy of: The Civil War Library and Museum, Philadelphia, Pa.

"WELL, JOHNNY, I GUESS YOU FELLOWS WILL GO HOME NOW TO STAY.

"LOOK HERE, YANK, YOU *GUESS*, DO YOU, THAT WE FELLOWS ARE GOING HOME TO STAY? MAYBE WE ARE. BUT DON'T BE GIVING US ANY OF YOUR IMPUDENCE. IF YOU DO, WE'LL COME BACK AND LICK YOU AGAIN."

Union and Confederate veterans at Appomattox

Veterans groups became a powerful political force in the years after the war. Amongst these surviving members of the 23d Ohio gathering 20 years after the Confederate surrender is former president Rutherford B. Hayes (center).

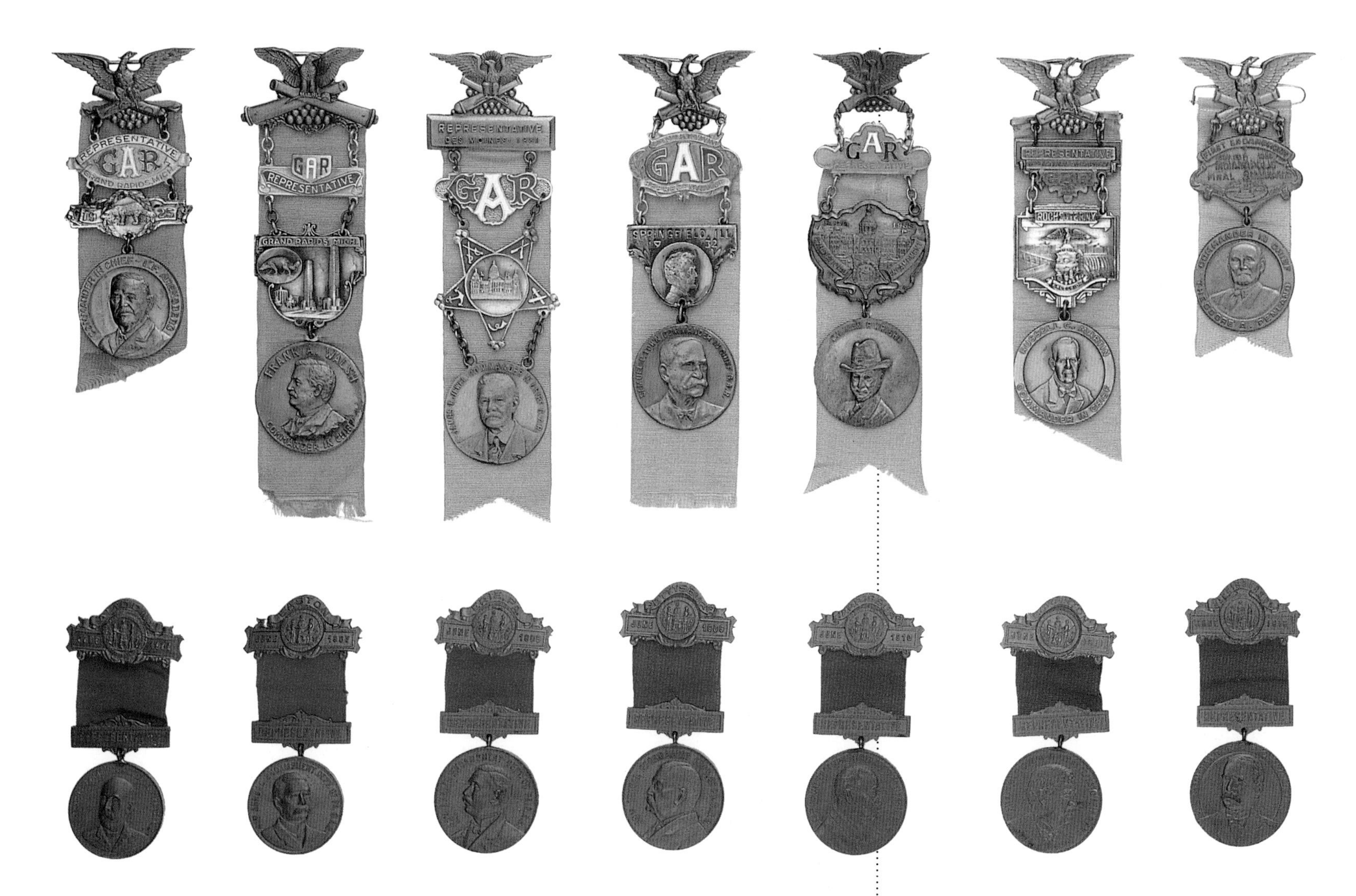

A selection of badges celebrating National Encampments of the Grand Army of the Republic. Throughout the immediate post-war years, the GAR was the official voice of the hundreds of thousands of Union veterans.
Artifacts courtesy of: The Civil War Library and Museum, Philadelphia, Pa.

With America reunited and growing rapidly, there was too much to do to keep alive the old hatreds. Respect came first, then admiration, and in after years nostalgia and romanticism, all to blur and then diffuse their differences. By 1896, when the Democratic Party split, one faction nominated Union General John M. Palmer for the Presidency, and as his running mate *Confederate* General Simon B. Buckner. Two years later, when America went to war with Spain, one-time Confederate generals donned the blue to fight side-by-side with their old foes. Reconciliation may have been slow, but it came in less time than it had taken for the old animosities to bring them to war in the first place. However adept they had been at killing one another, Americans simply were never very good at hating each other.

Index

Page references for illustrations are in *italics*. Quotations are indicated by *q*.

BIBLIOGRAPHY

Bruce Catton, *A Stillness at Appomattox,* New York, 1953

Edward M. Coffman, *The Old Army,* New York, 1986

Burke Davis, *The Civil War, Strange and Fascinating Facts,* New York, 1982

William C. Davis, *Breckinridge: Statesman, Soldier, Symbol, Baton Rouge, 1974*

William C. Davis, *The Orphan Brigade,* New York, 1980

Benjamin W. Jones, *Under the Stars and Bars,* Dayton, Ohio, 1975

E.B. Long, *The Civil War Day by Day,* New York, 1987

James M. McPherson, *Battle Cry of Freedom,* New York, 1985

James M. McPherson, *Ordeal by Fire,* New York, 1982

Bell I. Wiley, *The Common Soldier of the Civil War,* New York, 1975

Bell I. Wiley, *The Life of Johnny Reb,* Indianapolis, Ind, 1943

Bell I. Wiley, *The Life of Billy Yank,* Indianapolis, Ind, 1951

PICTURE CREDITS

The publishers have endeavored to ensure that both the still photographs and the artifacts in this book are correctly credited. Should any illustration in this book be incorrectly attributed, the publisher apologizes.

Some references to picture sources have been abbreviated as follows: Library of Congress: LC; US Military History Institute: USMHI; US National Archives: NA; Salamander Books: SB

Front endpaper: USMHI; 1: Lloyd Ostendorf Collection; 2-3: NA; 4: Americana Image Gallery; 7: William Gladstone; 8: SB; 10: SB; 11: SB; 12: LC; 13: NA; 14: Burton Historical Collection, Detroit Public LIbrary; 15: Dale S. Snair Collection; 16: (left) NA, (right) Spencer H. Watterson, Pontiac, Il; 18: (both) SB; 21: (left) Valentine Museum, Richmond, Va, (right) SB; 22: SB; 23: NA; 24: (left) Herb Peck, (right) West Virginia University, Morganstown; 25: Lloyd Ostendorf Collection; 26: NA; 27: SB; 28: (left) Mass MOLLUS, (right) SB; 31: (left) Minnesota Historical Society, (right) Robert McDonald; 32, 33: SB; 34: Museum of the Confederacy, Richmond, Va; 35: NA; 37: Ronn Palm; 38: Joe Carole, Jr; 41: SB; 43, 44: SB; 45: NA; 46: International Museum of Photography, George Eastman House; 47: NA; 48, 49: SB; 50: T. Scott Sanders; 52: Mass MOLLUS; 54: NA; 57: (left) Rudolf K. Haerle, (right) Ronn Palm; 58: NA; 61: SB; 62: Kean Archives, Philadelphia, Pa; 64: USMHI; 65: SB; 66: LC; 69, 71: SB; 72: Chicago Historical Society; 73: Robert L. Kotchian; 74: NA; 75: SB; 76: (both) SB; 78: (top) International Msseum of Photography, George Eastman House, (main picture) SB; 80, 81, 83: SB; 84: USMHI; 85: NA; 86, 87, 89 (both): SB; 90, 91: SB; 92: Chicago Historical Society; 93: SB; 94: USMHI; 95: SB; 96: USMHI; 97: University of Georgia Libraries, Athens, Ga; 98: Americana Image Gallery; 99: Burton J. Austin; 100, 101: SB; 102: USMHI; 103: LC; 104: Chicago Historical Society; 105: SB; 107: NA; 108: SB; 110: NA; 112, 115: SB; 116: NA; 119: (both) SB; 121, 122, 123: NA; 124: SB; 126, 127: NA; 129; 127, 131: SB; 133, 134: NA; 137: (left) Kentucky Historical Institute, (right) SB; 138-139, 140: SB; Back endpaper: Kentucky Historical Society.

MAJOR CIVIL WAR COLLECTIONS

Ancient and Honorable Artillery Company Armory
Faneuil Hall
Boston, MA 02109

Atlanta Historical Society
3101 Andrews Drive
N.W. Atlanta, Ga 30305

Augusta-Richmond County Museum
540 Telfair Street
Augusta, Ga 30901

Casemate Museum
Fort Monroe, Va 23651

Chicago Historical Society
Clark Street at North Avenue
Chicago, Il 60614

Chickamauga-Chattanooga National Military Park
Fort Oglethorpe, Ga 30742

Civil War Library and Museum
1805 Pine Street
Philadelphia, Pa 19103

Confederate Museum
Alexander Street
Crawfordville, Ga 30631

Confederate Museum
929 Camp Street
New Orleans, La 70130

Confederate Naval Museum
201 4th Street
Columbus, Ga 31902

Fredericksburg and Spotsylvania National Military Park
120 Chatham Lane
Fredericksburg, Va 22405

Fort Ward Museum and Historic Site
4301 W. Braddock Road
Alexandria, Va 22304

Gettysburg National Military Park
Gettysburg, Pa 17325

Grand Army of the Republic Memorial Hall Museum
State Capitol
419 N. Madison, WI 53702

Kentucky Military History Museum
Old State Arsenal
East Main Street, Frankfort, Ky 40602

Milwaukee Public Museum
800 W. Wells Street
Milwaukee, WI 53233

Smithsonian Institution
National Museum of American History
900 Jefferson Drive
S.W. Washington, DC 20560

South Carolina Confederate Relic Room and Museum
World War Memorial Building
920 Sumter Street,
Columbia, SC 29201

Springfield Armory National Historic Site
1 Armory Square
Springfield, MA 01105

State Historical Museum of Wisconsin
30 North Carroll Street
Madison, WI 53703

The Confederate Museum
188 Meeting Street
Charleston, SC 29401

The Museum of the Confederacy
1201 E. Clay Street
Richmond, Va 23219

US Army Military History Institute
Carlisle Barracks, Pa 17013

Virginia Historical Society
428 North Boulevard
Richmond, Va 23221

VMI Museum
Virginia Military Institute
Jackson Memorial Hall
Lexington, Va 24450

Warren Rifles Confederate Museum
95 Chester Street
Front Royal, Va 22630

War Memorial Museum of Virginia
9285 Warwick Blvd.
Huntingdon Park
Newport News, Va 23607

West Point Museum
United States Military Academy
West Point, NY 10996

ICE CREAM